The Benedictine Gift to Music

The Benedictine Gift to Music

Katharine Le Mée

PAULIST PRESS
New York/Mahwah, N.J.

Book design by Celine M. Allen

Cover design by Diego Linares

Library of Congress Cataloging-in-Publication Data

Le Mée, Katharine W.
    The Benedictine gift to music / Katharine Le Mée
            p. cm.
Includes bibliographical references and index.
    ISBN 0-8091-4178-7 (alk. paper)
    1. Gregorian chant—History and criticism. 2. Gregorian chant—Influence.
3. Benedictines—Music—History and criticism. 4. Benedictines—Influence.
5. Music— History and criticism. I. Title.
    ML3082 .L36 2003
    782.32'22—dc21

                                                                    2003007747

Published by Paulist Press
997 Macarthur Boulevard
Mahwah, New Jersey 07430

www.paulistpress.com

Printed and bound in the
United States of America

Contents

That in all things God may be glorified.

Acknowledgments

The idea of having a book that would celebrate the contributions of the Order of St. Benedict to the development of Western sacred music originated with Abbot Marcel Rooney, O.S.B., former abbot primate of the worldwide Benedictine Confederation. I would like to thank him for launching me on the life-transforming adventure occasioned by the writing of this book. I particularly appreciate the exacting and careful scholarship he brought to the reading of my manuscript and the generous, open-hearted encouragement he offered along the way—qualities that I value as preeminently Benedictine.

Surely this book would not have been written without the never-failing and extremely knowledgeable guidance of Fr. Abbot Patrick Barry, O.S.B. Through his gift for finding exactly the right reference at exactly the right time and through his close reading of my text at every stage, he watched over the intellectual development of the book. More important even than this invaluable support were his continuing prayers to God on my behalf, demonstrating so clearly the meaning of participation in the mystical body of Christ. Abbot Barry's new translation of St. Benedict's Rule and his written reflections upon it and upon the Benedictine model of education have offered me profound insight into the meaning of leading a life inspired by St. Benedict amidst the challenges of today's world.

Special thanks are due as well to other Benedictine friends who introduced me to their way of life and prayer, thus enabling my book to be more than words: Sr. Donald Corcoran, O.S.B. (Cam.), for offering me her love, scholarship, and intense interest in the world of Spirit; Fr. Ralph Wright, O.S.B., for sharing his hymns, poetry, and humor and for his deft ferreting out of insidious errors in my text; Sr. Delores Dufner, O.S.B., for her careful reading of my manuscript from the musical point of view and for the gracious welcome she and others offered me at St. Benedict's Monastery in St. Joseph, Minnesota.

I would also like to thank Yuval Waldman for a number of conversations exploring the relationship between Gregorian chant and the development of Western sacred music and express my admiration for the work of Johannes Somary and Stephen Perillo who, through composing a new *Te Deum* and a new *Magnificat* respectively, have shown that the Benedictine influence is still alive and vibrant in contemporary sacred music.

Deep appreciation is offered to my husband, Jean Le Mée, who has offered me the fruits of his keen understanding of the medieval world, unending patience in going over so many drafts of this book, and a continuing supply of love, devotion, and good cheer. Our daughter, Hannah Le Mée, has kept me spiritually alive and alert through her questions and desire to know about the world behind and beyond appearances.

Finally, a word of profound gratitude to friends who have ministered to me in ways spiritual, companionable, and material: Toinette Lippe, Solveig Dale Eskedahl, Alice Worth, Volker Stutzer, Astrid Fitzgerald, and André Bénaroya. I very much appreciate as well the enthusiasm for my manuscript expressed by Fr. Lawrence Boadt and for the efficient and expert handling and editing of it by Paul McMahon, both of Paulist Press.

Preface

This work is being published at a time characterized by a new interest in the plainchant musical form. This interest is being manifested even by many persons who have never had the experience of hearing the plainchant performed within its place of origin, the Roman Catholic liturgy. Rather, this unusual music is being appreciated for its inherent musical qualities as well as the profound effect it can have on the psyche of the listener or performer.

It is timely, then, to probe more deeply into the origins of the plainchant, in particular the Benedictine monastic origins from which arose so much of the extant material available today that contains this music. The author takes pains to bring out the importance of the Benedictine monks for the notation and the theory of the plainchant, as well as its earliest instrumental accompaniment. But one cannot help but be struck by the fact that there is much more than history here. In addition to that data, we are introduced to something of the mysticism that may be seen to underlie the music. It may be that the extensive development of what might be called "the mysticism of the octave" will surprise many readers. With this, Le Mée wants to acquaint us with some of the inner spirit that is expressed in this form of song.

That inner spirit has been embodied very vibrantly in Benedictine monastic life and liturgy. This helps to explain the paradox of a music which when sung really expresses the spirit of silence; which with almost wordless vocalization really attempts to express the very word of God; which with the action of singing really is meant to be a vehicle for contemplation. The author has understood the paradox inherent in the monastic life itself and has tried to show the effect that that life has had on the greatest music to come from that milieu. As Benedictine monastic life has perdured for a millennium and a half, one cannot but hope that the music that says so much about that life might have an equally long and enduring effect. Thanks are due the author for her efforts to probe the past of the plainchant, so that it might be appreciated yet more deeply in the future.

Abbot Marcel Rooney, O.S.B.
Former Abbot Primate of the Benedictine Confederation

1
Benedictine Identity

"Hear God's call and answer."
St. Benedict

Gregorian Chant

There is a song reaching the whole earth, wrought from patience, love, and prayer. Neither violent nor assertive, it is peace begetting peace, love made manifest. Listen to it with the ear of your heart; let it go deep within. Open to the sound, to the holy words, to the life of which it sings.

Ancient, yet carrying with it new resonance and beauty, a clear, peaceful, and spirit-filled song keeps bringing healing and love to a world torn apart by violence, grief, and fear. This song, Gregorian chant, is singing and praying itself into our listening awareness. Its history reaches back to Christianity's earliest centuries, when followers of Jesus first began to remember their Lord at regular times during the day and far into the night. Its life extends across fifteen centuries, always keeping its own integrity while inspiring unending creativity as music of many parts developed out of its single unharmonized line.

Gregorian chant is a calm and peaceful melody that gives musical expression to Holy Scripture, very often the psalms. Its very essence is profoundly spiritual, centering the mind and heart in God alone, making it the perfect musical prayer of the Christian Church. Those of us accustomed to more complexity of rhythm, tone, and harmony may question the value of a musical expression that appears so simple and unadorned. The claim that the whole of Western music could have its origin in so humble a source seems, on the face of it, to be a rank impossibility. We are accustomed to power creating power, to abundance, to fanfare and clash of cymbals as heralds of the new and creative endeavor. And yet the very birth of Christ, "in lowly estate," provides a powerful reminder of the fact that true spirituality and creativity begin not with loud speaking and acquisition of many things but in the heart of a person receptive to God's still, small voice within.

Chant calls us to mindfulness, to the realization that we are, in our essence, at one with God and that that unity is the source of our creativity and of our healing, both personal and collective. The worship experience that it embodies is never purely personal. Rather, it involves community—the body of Christ praying daily and hourly across the world—where each person is fully present and yet where no one seeks to occupy center stage to the detriment of anyone else. Gregorian chant brings its singers and listeners into the present moment, which is full of joy and peace, yet stripped of all reference to anything worldly, anything distracting from worship, prayer, and praise. Its purpose is to remind, through the medium of the human voice, that God is all, in all.

Prior to the Second Vatican Council, convened in the early 1960s by Pope John XXIII and completed by Pope Paul VI,

Gregorian chant found its most appropriate place in the Roman Catholic High Mass and in the regular sung prayer of the monasteries. On these occasions liturgical texts were sung in Latin, rather than in the vernacular languages of the worshipers. Therefore, the experience was for many a powerful source of nourishment for the heart rather than for the intellect. The chant was there to bring singers and listeners into an awe-filled awareness of the presence of Christ.

Since the early 1990s, when the Gregorian chant recording of the Benedictine monks of Santo Domingo de Silos spread across the world, attracting more than six million listeners in more than forty countries, this tranquil and radiant music has been featured in countless other CDs recorded in the United States and abroad. Made aware of its calming yet stimulating effect through the research of French physician Alfred Tomatis, American sound expert Don Campbell, and others, many have recognized the power of chant to offer healing to body, mind, and spirit. People of all faiths are now using these thousand-year-old melodies as a source of quiet and refreshment. Therapists and doctors play them in their offices to help patients relax and overcome their fears.

With the liturgical innovations encouraged by the Second Vatican Council and its overall effort to offer both to clergy and laypeople an opportunity to participate more easily in worship services, a movement away from Latin and consequently away from the singing of Gregorian chant took place. However, with the passage of time, which brought with it musical innovation and, in some cases, new inspiration, there has been a revived interest in chant, both in the context of Roman Catholic worship and among spiritually minded people in general.

The Benedictines

Although the chanting of Holy Scripture by Christians dates from the earliest centuries after the earthly life of Christ, its clearest and most persistent advocate was St. Benedict, who was born in Italy in 480. Through instructions clearly given in his famous Rule, St. Benedict established the prayerful singing of the psalms as the quintessential element of monastic Christian worship. If he were living today he would certainly counsel us never to let go of prayer, sung or spoken, to keep it as the atmosphere in which we live, to create a community of believers who pray, to sing with enthusiasm and without mistakes, and to do honor to the Lord through our timeliness, our attention, and our heartfelt participation.

The Benedictines, or followers of St. Benedict, are a group of men and women mainly within the Roman Catholic Church[1] who have chosen to devote themselves primarily to the quest for God rather than to any other specific work. Those who are monks or nuns generally reside in communities called monasteries or convents, though some live a solitary or an eremitical life as hermits; still others, the oblates, continue to live in the secular world while maintaining a close connection with the religious community.

Benedictines perform many different types of work, but the specific task is always secondary to the primary emphasis: to live the teachings of Jesus Christ completely and wholeheartedly. Specifically, this means the active cultivation of God's presence in every aspect of human life, personally through daily prayer and study of Holy Scripture and collectively through communal worship and service. Persons who join the Order are fully committed to a Christ-centered life and, through the example of their daily witness, remind others to be less caught up in the things of the world. Abbot Marcel Rooney, O.S.B., expressed this idea when he said:

> The Order is a sign in the world of the primary impor-tance of God in human life or, put in other more philo-sophical terms, of the primary importance of *transcen-dence*. No matter how mundane or exalted the work a Benedictine does, God pervades all of our life, if we are faithful to our calling and Rule. Thus there is a witness-ing contrast between our lives and the lives of those who are devoted primarily to advancing an egocentric and godless humanism, or those who would divinize technol-ogy, money, or power. "In God alone be at rest, my soul," says the Psalmist—and Benedictines strive to live that verse fully.[2]

In a world where the unimportant is called important, where distraction is rampant and people have difficulty in distinguish-ing between one thing and another, often leveling everything to the lowest common denominator—in a word, where most are spiritually asleep—the Benedictines watch over society, remind-ing it of the reality and truth of God's presence and love.

It has therefore been the traditional vocation of Benedictine monastics to faithfully chant the Holy Scriptures day in and day out since the days of St. Benedict. The timing of the Opus Dei (or "Divine Office"), devoted to remembering God in prayer throughout the day, has never been left to the whims and moods of individuals. Rather, prayer periods have been very carefully and specifically structured. A monastery is first and foremost a place for remembering God's presence and power, and no detail in the carrying out of worship should ever be neglected.

Not all Benedictines are musically adept and, for some, the task of singing this deeply unified and self-revelatory chant can present a severe challenge. However, it is not the technique that is primary. Rather, it is each monastic's intimate link to the Creator of all life that inspires the song, giving it such beauty. Chant sung in the concert hall, rather than in the church, never nourishes in quite the same way. It literally depends on its sacred context.

This peaceful, refreshing chant has shown astonishing power in the way that it has been used to enhance communal worship in the creation of liturgies for the Mass and the monastic hours. Further, it has provided the very foundation for all of Western sacred polyphonic music—the Mozart Requiem, the Bach B-minor Mass, Palestrina's tightly woven counterpoint, Handel's *Messiah*. All of these magnificent choral masterpieces can be traced back to a simple and humble monastic origin in the chant.

As this book will explain, Gregorian chant has developed in two musical dimensions: horizontally through the appending or insertion of elaborate enhancements and vertically through the addition of many parts with rhythms and harmonies as diverse as human inspiration can provide. Through the centuries, it has passed into many different cultures, taking on color and renewed vigor according to the spiritual needs of time and place. The chant is one of the greatest of musical achievements. However, it is vital to remember that it is never simply a "work of art," existing only for the beauty that it embodies within itself. It is the product of a lived, communal, and sacred culture finding its true meaning in Christian liturgy and worship. It has evolved out of a way of life centered in Christ and in the experience of the monastic community.[3]

The Beginnings of Chant

To understand the origins of Gregorian chant, we may picture in our minds the very earliest gatherings of Christian worshipers coming together in praise of the risen Christ. Legend has it that melodies, finding their source both in informal Hebrew worship and in the religious practice of the East, may have filtered their way into the experience of the early Christian Church. Though little is known about the actual sound of the music used, we may suppose that, at first, the words of scripture were simply intoned on a single note or simple melody and that gradually, over time, the repertoire increased, adding borrowings and innovations.

Music was a powerful unifying force holding and beautifying the holy words of scripture and magnifying the intent toward God of the Christian community. The effect produced by the group was much stronger than that of the individual worshiper. What was sung was remembered, better engraved into peoples' hearts than the spoken word. Very specific times of the day were chosen for this purposeful recalling not only of the words of Hebrew Scripture but also of the events in the life of Jesus. People instinctively knew the value of persistent, regular prayer—a habit taken up by thousands today who, following early Christian practice, pray at fixed hours of the day and night.

The early church father Tertullian[4] attests to the fact that, as early as the second century, monks in Carthage (now Tunis in North Africa) were already chanting in the morning, in the late afternoon, and during the night, while private individuals were coming together for worship at three-hour intervals during the day. Other written records[5] say that during the third century hymn singing was popular, as well as the chanting of psalms.

There is abundant evidence[6] that St. Ambrose (340–397) introduced psalmody and hymns into worship services in Milan during the fourth century and that the Spanish nun Etheria made a pilgrimage to Jerusalem and returned with a detailed report about chant practices already in place there.

The liturgy, or form and arrangement that over the years Christian worship assumed, was repetitive year by year. In the same way that hours of prayer would recur at certain times of the day, festivals and celebrations would repeat themselves each year. An early Roman calendar dated 336 already indicates December 25 as the date to commemorate Christ's birth. Four weeks of preparation, known as Advent, were planned to precede the festival. After Christmas there were the celebrations of Epiphany, Easter, Ascension, and Pentecost. The pattern included six months when Christ's life was modeled, followed by six more months when additional time was afforded for reflection on and practice of his teaching.[7]

A vital part of the developing liturgy was the Mass itself, the ritual enactment of Christ's Last Supper with his disciples, when he told them that he would be present with them whenever they celebrated the Eucharist in his memory, that their sins would be forgiven, and that, after their earthly life, they would enjoy eternal life with him forever.

By the time of St. Benedict, the music both of the daily hours of prayer and the Mass was quite well developed. The hours consisted mainly of chanted psalms, hymns, and prayers, whereas the Mass was a commemoration and participation in the eucharistic or Last Supper celebration. No one can really tell the specific sound of the melodies or the exact way in which they were sung. Most probably the chants represented the work of many anonymous composers and singers working for several centuries before Benedict and several centuries afterward.

One thing is nevertheless certain, and that is that St. Benedict saw the regular chanting of psalms—the purposeful remembrance of God in prayer—as a work exceeding all others in importance. In the Rule he provided a seasonal schedule of how the psalmody was to be done and an arrangement of psalms that was flexible and amenable to change. Not subject to compromise, however, was the principle that the whole Psalter of 150 psalms was to be recited each week and that the cycle should begin again on Sunday during the night hours. "Any monastic community which chants less than the full Psalter with the usual canticles each week," said Benedict, "shows clearly that it is too indolent in its service of God. After all, we read that our holy Fathers had the energy to fulfill in one single day what we in our lukewarm devotion only aspire to complete in a whole week."[8]

These words indicate that Benedict was very aware of the chant tradition practiced in monasteries for centuries before his own time. His important contribution was to bring order and regularity to the practice. Like everything else that he prescribed, the daily program of chanted prayers was challenging, but not so much as to be impossible for a person sufficiently motivated.

At regular, seasonally determined intervals during the day and once during the night, the sound of chant could be heard in Benedict's abbey church of Montecassino—psalms beginning and ending with antiphons or short verses of scripture, Ambrosian hymns, alleluias, and the frequent punctuation of the *Gloria Patri*, during which the monks would rise from their benches and bow in reverence for the Holy Trinity. One of the monks would serve as cantor; the others would respond in unison. The *Te Deum* and the *Magnificat,* texts still inspiring musical composition today, were regularly sung.

This impetus offered to the world by St. Benedict and his monks quite literally put the song in the air. Since that time, Benedictines across the centuries have always renewed its sound, each and every day, keeping it there as the center of their own worship experience and making it available in mind and heart as a resource for musicians and composers to draw upon. Wherever there are Benedictines, the chant is present, glorifying God and inviting worshipers to draw near to Christ.

For two centuries after the life of St. Benedict, the Roman Catholic liturgy greatly expanded. It is not easy to identify any specific composers or liturgists behind this flowering. One thing is certain, however, and that is that St. Gregory the Great, St. Benedict's only biographer and the most influential of medieval popes, took a great interest in the chant repertory that bears his name. Although most probably not a composer, Pope Gregory I is credited with editing a famous cycle of chants for the liturgical year, establishing the famous Roman *schola cantorum* (school of singers), and mandating the use of the *Alleluia* in the Mass for the entire year, except for the period of Lent. This outstanding pope was also preeminently responsible for the spread of the chant liturgy on the European continent and, most especially, to England.

The Growth of Chant

We can only marvel at the way in which the chant repertory for the Mass, the monastic hours, and the liturgical year was organized by Pope Gregory and others. A tradition that may have helped these early liturgists concerns the musical octave. Linked with wisdom schools through the ages, from the Egyptians and Greeks to the Romans,[9] it provided a model useful in organizing all significant events, from the architectural arrangement of houses of worship and the composition of literary works to the organization of ceremonies in the monastery and church. This model is more than just intellectual and visual; the effect of its progression is known experientially through listening and singing.

The octave, very familiar today, consists of eight notes—*Do, Re, Mi, Fa, Sol, La, Si (Ti), Do*—each contributing a specific quality to the progression. The intervals between *Mi* and *Fa* and *Si* and *Do*, half steps, are different from the intervals between the other notes, which are whole steps, and they require special attention in singing so that the octave proceeds normally and does not go off course. These two elements of the octave—the subjective quality of each note when sung in sequence and the requirements of the two intervals unequal to the others—provide an analog to the progression of significant events. Later chapters will make clear how this analogy may be seen in the arrangement of the stages of the Mass, in the monastic hours, and in the arrangement of liturgical celebrations across the year.

During the seventh and eighth centuries, a time when the Latin world was falling apart, only the Christian monasteries kept the light of culture burning by forming communities where chant and other manuscripts saved from antiquity were kept and some of the learning stayed alive. During this period, Benedictine missionaries carried the chant throughout Western Europe and several regional variations of the Christian liturgy thus developed— Mozarabic on the Iberian Peninsula, Gallican in Gaul, Ambrosian in Milan, German in Leipzig and Aachen, and Roman in Rome—

each with its own particular flavor. It is important to note, however, that even though the chant survives in thousands of manuscripts from many countries over the course of many centuries, it is astonishingly uniform; local variations occurring from one area of Europe to another are generally relatively minor. Through the creative effort at composition of the Benedictine monks and nuns in all these countries, the repertory amazingly increased to include nearly four thousand chants for the church year.

Bede's *Ecclesiastical History of the English People* chronicles a crucial episode in the history of the chant in mid-seventh century. It concerns Abbot John, clearly himself a monk, who was arch-cantor of St. Peter's in Rome. Benet Biscop (ex–war lord and converted monk and founder of Wearmouth and Jarrow) "borrowed" him from the Pope and brought him to Britain to teach his monks the chant, and all the other monks of Britain came to learn from him also. This momentous occasion is described as follows:

> Benedict received Abbot John and conducted him to Britain, where he was to teach his monks the chant for the liturgical year as it was sung at Saint Peter's, Rome. In accordance with the Pope's instructions, Abbot John taught the cantors of the monastery the theory and practice of singing and reading aloud, and he put into writing all that was necessary for the proper observance of festivals throughout the year. This document is still preserved in this monastery, and many copies have been made for other places. John's instruction was not limited to the brethren of this monastery alone; for men who were proficient singers came from nearly all the monas-

teries of the province to hear him, and he received many invitations to teach elsewhere.[10]

This was probably the beginning of the chant in the British Isles.

Musicologists, in their study of chant manuscripts of the ninth and tenth centuries, have found clear indications of the chant used in the liturgy of the Western Church. The signs in these manuscripts are not true written musical notes but rather depictions of shapes to be traced in the air by the hand of the conductor. Their direction reminded the *schola*, members of the singing school, who were singing from memory, of the melody and clearly indicated both rhythm and ornamentation. These manuscripts are very important, since they probably reflect a seventh-century reformation of the yet earlier Gregorian chant (all of which was lost in its original form), since no musical notation yet existed.

Historical evidence shows that, beginning with the reign of Pope Vitalian (657–672) the liturgical music of the papal court was significantly renewed. The chants had become burdened with extraneous notes that tended to blur the melodic line, rendering it less clear. The pope and his court decided to remedy the situation. Under their influence and probably with the help of Byzantine musicians, the chants were restored to something more resembling their ancient form. From these efforts came a renewed chant remarkable in its rhythmic approach, composed in a free rhythm of long and short notes set in a 2:1 proportion. This rhythm, sometimes called "proportional," was particularly well adapted to coincide with the accentual patterning of the Latin language itself and provided great subtlety and variety in its expression.[11] This chant was regularly offered in the pope's private chapel and on days of special celebration when the pope and his court would travel to certain other churches in Rome, where they would sing the new liturgical chant.

In the eighth century a political rapprochement between Pepin, king of the Franks from 751, and his son Charlemagne, crowned emperor in Rome in 800, with the papacy resulted in wide dissemination throughout the Holy Roman Empire of this proportional chant as it had come to be practiced in Rome. Charlemagne saw common forms of worship as a way of uniting his vast empire. He considered himself the divinely appointed ruler of a chosen people, whose liturgical customs had to approach the ideals represented by the usage of the papacy in Rome. He therefore requested that trained singers be sent from Rome north to Gaul (today's northern France) to visit his court. The cities of Rouen, Metz, and Chartres in France and St. Gall in Switzerland were particularly receptive, welcoming the teachers who would train their monks. This proportional chant so admired by Charlemagne and practiced at his insistence throughout his empire reached its zenith in the tenth century and began to decline in the eleventh. A medium best suited to either a trained soloist or a *schola cantorum*, its complex rhythms proved unsuitable for singing by most monastic choirs. The clear differentiation of long and short notes so essential to the Carolingian chant gradually gave way to a manner of singing that equalized the rhythmical value of the notes.

Benedictines as Musical Liturgists

From the seventh to the eleventh centuries, music came to occupy a place of greater and greater importance for Benedict's followers. As Benedictinism became virtually synonymous with Western ecclesiastical culture, any new musical achievements also necessarily became Benedictine. The chant was first notated in Benedictine manuscripts and the final development of Gregorian chant took place within Benedictine monasteries.

By the time of Charlemagne, certain monks had abandoned manual labor altogether, having become clerical choristers rather than lay monks. As such, they regarded the singing of the liturgy as their central task. This process reached its zenith in the tenth century in monastic centers such as Cluny.

Most influential as a center of liturgical innovation, the Abbey of Cluny in Burgundy occupied a central position in Christendom from its foundation in 910 throughout the whole medieval period. Its astute founder, in order to protect it from the depredations of local barons, placed it entirely under the authority of the Holy See. That action gave its monks the ability to develop a distinct form of monasticism in which manual labor and everything else gradually was absorbed by the liturgy. Cluny was directly linked with the church of Rome and came into existence at a time when the centers of learning founded by the Carolingians in cathedrals and monasteries were in overall decline. Under the leadership of a remarkable succession of abbots, Cluny's influence spread through France and Spain.

Raoul Glaber, a Benedictine monk and chronicler from the eleventh century, wrote that the very great number (400) of monks in residence at Cluny allowed Masses to be celebrated constantly from the earliest hours of the day until the hours assigned for rest; he added that they went about it with so much dignity and veneration that one would think they were angels rather than men. This intense liturgical activity favored many forms of musical innovation and the addition of more and more yearly celebrations. By that time the singing of the liturgy is said to have required about eight hours on a normal day and longer on Sundays and feast days. Many changes were made in the original Benedictine liturgy and the Mass itself was expanded, as will be explained in chapter 7, to include tropes, sequences, and other compositions far exceeding the length and complexity of the original chants. The secular (i.e., non-monastic) cathedrals and churches generally conformed to monastic usage and widely accepted these liturgical additions. Certain of these, such as the Office of the Dead and the Office and Mass of the Blessed Virgin Mary, were of great importance for late medieval polyphony.

One of the most creative of medieval composers, and the first composer whose biography is known in considerable detail, was Benedictine abbess Hildegard of Bingen (1098–1179). Visionary, artist, poet, and counsel to the pope, Hildegard is responsible for a large corpus of chant, created, she said, by divine inspiration. Applying unprecedented artistic innovation to the composition of works intended for the choir of her abbey church, Hildegard produced chants of stunning originality, only fully researched and appreciated in the last twenty-five years.

The feminine influence is also seen in the power of the Virgin Mary to inspire Benedictine monks and nuns. In "Our Lady," as she is called, they see the example of perfect obedience to the will of the Father, a source of comfort and solace. Her influence has inspired so much monastic musical creativity that we shall devote a whole chapter to it.

Benedictine Music Theorists

Aside from the liturgy and the chant, there are three Benedictine musical achievements of great importance: the establishment of music theory, the development of ecclesiastical vocal polyphony, and the introduction of the pipe organ into the church.

Music theory of the fifth and sixth centuries, inherited from the Greco-Roman tradition, even when expounded by Christian musical theorists, remained largely a mathematical discipline based on numerical ratios and proportions. Basically it had little influence on actual musical composition or performance. However, Benedictine theorists of the period from the ninth to the eleventh centuries such as Aurelian, Hucbald, Pseudo-Odo, and Hermannus Contractus, while remaining interested in the mathematical aspects, took the crucial step of applying the theory to actual practice. In particular, they worked out fundamental concepts such as the modal system patterned after the Greek modes.

But the great innovation that was to distinguish Western music and allow its explosive development through subsequent centuries was the invention of notation. The need for notation that would allow chant to be passed on and performed uniformly by all monasteries began to be met by an unknown monk who had the idea of using neumes—dots, hooks, and small strokes—that indicated the general up and down pattern of the melody but not its tonal pitch or the length of its notes. Toward the end of the tenth century, the notation was changed to symbols on lines that also indicated the pitch of the tone. At first only one line was used; then more were added. The number of lines varied until Camaldolese Benedictine Guido d'Arezzo, who lived from the end of the tenth to the beginning of the eleventh century, suggested that the same notes be placed permanently on specified lines and spaces. He is credited with the development of the four-line staff, which became the standard staff for Gregorian chant.[12]

The earliest efforts at notated polyphony, also the work of Benedictines, flowered in England with the Winchester Troper (a troper being a collection of chants extended by original musical composition and additional words) and in France with the Troper of St. Martial of Limoges associated with the motherhouse of Cluny.

During the tenth century, the pipe organ, which had appeared in the West in 757 and been used by monastic teachers to illustrate the mathematical laws underlying pitch relationships, began to be found in abbey churches with increased frequency.

Decreased Benedictine Influence followed by Rebirth

During the latter part of the twelfth century, musical leadership passed from Benedictine monastics to musicians associated with the great cathedrals of Western Europe, where modal and intensely rhythmic polyphony was extensively developed by theorists such as Johannes de Garlandia, Franco of Cologne, and Léonin and his successor, Pérotin, at the Cathedral of Notre Dame in Paris. From the remaining centuries of the Middle Ages until the nineteenth century, Benedictinism remained to some extent outside the mainstream of musical composition, but it always continued its role as preserver of the chant. In late medieval England, where many of the great cathedrals like Canterbury, Durham, and Winchester were also Benedictine abbeys, endowed chapels were constructed and monastics were trained by secular musicians to chant polyphonic Masses and offices.

In spite of the somewhat decreased influence of monasticism in general and its creative expression in music in particular from the fifteenth through the eighteenth centuries, certain abbeys continued to exercise a very strong influence.[13] The nineteenth century saw a monastic renaissance. Benedictines again came to the fore, channeling their artistry, creativity, and attention to detail into liturgical and music revivals. At the outset, these revivals were the product of the work of the Abbey of Solesmes in France, whose monastic scholarship and meticulous and inspired performance of the chant restored its place as the primary official music of the church, an astonishing story to be told in chapter 7. Other very significant work was done in Germany, particularly at the Abbey of Saint Martin in Beuron.

Gregorian chant, elaborated and retained by the Benedictines throughout the centuries, is the place where all Christian music begins. It is the connection between the song, however it may be rendered, and the unseen, divine world of causes. Its ancient melodies are capable of holding all our rejoicing and all our sorrow, our petitions, our questions, our yearning—making them all an offering to God.

Chant carries the words of Holy Scripture, acting as its perfect instrument. In the singing there is nothing that will excite our passions, nothing to force an interpretation, no dramatic effort that will take us away into dreams. If we are attentive and allow it to happen, the music draws us away from our habitual state of distraction, of persistent exteriority, of search for God where God cannot be found. Its pure, peaceful tones slowly lead us inward to a place of peace and awareness of the divine presence, an awareness that is full of potential, without judgment, and open to all that is creative and new. This kind of music never enslaves the mind or the emotions; it sets them free for their most natural and personal expression. The individual may draw from the Holy Scripture thoughts and feelings most fully appropriate personally in the moment. The composer may find inspiration for an opus never before imagined, as will be seen in later chapters, when the musical developments from chant are described in detail.

There is something else about chant that also contributes to its perfection as a model for Christian prayer and for the music of worship. The singing involves the individual—his or her intention toward God, attention to the meaning of the words, and proper mastery of the required technique—but it also involves the group in an experience capable of transcending anything the singer might do alone. Social but never gregarious, the chant obliges each person to join with others in prayer and praise, to sing in unison with them, to include them in awareness.

This book will explain chant's remarkable history through more than fifteen centuries. As we begin this journey through musical time, we may search for the reason why this music has provided the platform for such a magnificent profusion of sacred music. Perhaps the reason is the universality and detachment from ego that its performance requires. Perhaps it is the atmosphere of open quietness provided by the monastic ambiance that has contributed so much to its power. Perhaps it is simply the fact that it represents "the word of God singing,"[14] a fruitful return to God of what was God's from the beginning. We will have time to reflect as we continue the story.

2
The Foundations

"Be wise enough to build on a rock."
St. Benedict

Early Monasticism

Benedictinism begins, of course, with St. Benedict. In 1964, at the time of the physical rebuilding of his famous monastery at Montecassino, this humble man was proclaimed by Pope Paul VI to be "the principal, heavenly patron of the whole of Europe"—a title Benedict himself would probably have eschewed. Although his name is associated before any other with Christian monasticism, he was not its founder.

For centuries before the time of Benedict, many men and women living in the Middle Eastern desert (the desert fathers and mothers, known as Abbas and Ammas) had been embracing a life where all secular influences were stripped away, but the first person referred to as a *monk* (Greek *monachus*, "one, alone, solitary") was St. Anthony (ca. 251–356—yes, he lived to 105 years of age!). We know of him through a biography written in Greek by St. Athanasius (patriarch of the ancient Egyptian city of Alexandria) and subsequently translated into Latin. Athanasius's *Life of Anthony*, the first great work of Christian hagiography and the most important piece of literature about the monastic movement, describes a man who led an austere life of self denial. Well educated, Anthony became, through struggle against obstacles presented by the world, the flesh, and the devil, a person of great spiritual discernment, devoted to Christ above all else. From the end of the fourth century onward, Anthanasius's portrait of Anthony was an inspiration to monks throughout the East and West.

Another early monastic leader was St. Pachomius, born around 292, probably in Upper Egypt. A skilled organizer and devoted to the scriptures, he followed an inner voice instructing him to "reconcile humankind with God" by building a monastic community where monks could lead a life of prayer and service. This was one of the first examples of cenobitic or communal, spiritual life—not just a grouping of individuals around a spiritual father but a real fellowship of brothers.

St. Basil (329–379), bishop of Caesarea, a city in the middle of Cappadocia in Asia Minor (modern-day Turkey), was a brilliant scholar and defender of the faith. His excellent education and wide experience of the world and the church added to his knowledge of scripture and other Christian writings made him extremely well qualified to give the monastic movement in the Greek-speaking world a sound foundation. His influence was very far-reaching in the development of monastic communities.

Monasticism in North Africa was offered great impetus by Augustine, bishop of Hippo (354–430), who was also one of the first church fathers to insist on life in community and on common ownership of property as opposed to the Egyptian tradition of relationship of each individual to God via the spiritual leader. The monks under his supervision were said to have practiced psalmody, *lectio divina*, silence, simplicity of life, humility, obedience, chastity—observances and values later associated with monastic life.

The most influential founder of monasticism in Western Europe was John Cassian (360–435), a monk and ascetic living in southern Gaul (present-day France) and the first to introduce the rules of Eastern monasticism to the West. A well-educated man, Cassian visited the holy sites in Palestine and the Egyptian desert. After being ordained a priest in Rome, he founded two monasteries in Marseilles. His personal influence and his *Institutes* (concerning monastic life lived in community, illustrated by examples drawn from his own observation), and his *Conferences* (devoted to the eight principal obstacles to perfection encountered by monks: gluttony, impurity, covetousness, anger, dejection, accidie [ennui], vainglory, and pride) contributed greatly to the diffusion of monasticism in the West. St. Benedict later referred to Cassian in writing his Rule and ordered sections from the *Conferences* to be read daily in his monasteries.

The introduction of monasticism to Italy may be dated from about 340, when St. Athanasius visited Rome accompanied by the two Egyptian monks Ammon and Isidore, disciples of St. Anthony. The publication of the *Life of St. Anthony* and its translation into Latin spread the knowledge of Egyptian monasticism in the Italian peninsula. For this reason, Italy long retained a purely Eastern form of monastic observance.

Certainly Italian monasticism was in need of a man who could adapt it to Western needs and circumstances and give it a form different from that of the East. This person was St. Benedict, whose radical blending of holiness and hard work placed him at the very center of a movement that was to nurture and preserve Western civilization for the next six centuries.

It is highly likely that Benedict borrowed from the writings of other Christian monastics, such as St. Pachomius, St. Basil, St. Augustine, and John Cassian. His most important source is said to be the *Rule of the Master*, written anonymously two or three decades prior to the Rule, some say perhaps by Benedict himself at an earlier stage of his development and understanding. In any case, the purpose was not to produce something new but to collect, assimilate, and make available the accumulated wisdom of Eastern and Western predecessors. Because of its broadness of vision, its synthetic quality, and the compassionate and non-dictatorial way in which it is written, Benedict's Rule gradually supplanted all others.

Benedict of Nursia

History and legend about the person of St. Benedict of Nursia come to us uniquely and directly from *The Dialogues* of St. Gregory the Great, who was inspired by Benedict and who equals him in importance. From this history of the lives of saints, and in particular the *Second Dialogue* or *Vita* ("life" in Latin), we learn of Benedict's deeds, his prophecies and reflections, and the miracles that abounded in his presence. We can also gain insight into his character, beliefs, and way of life from reading what he himself teaches in the Rule. There are no other extant sources.

Benedict was born in the Umbrian town of Nursia, high in the mountains northeast of Rome, in 480. Although not known primarily as a scholar, he studied briefly in Rome before retreating in disgust from the distracting and decadent society he observed there.

Turning his back on the promise of a successful career in business or government, he departed from worldly pursuits and moved to a secluded village about forty miles from Rome at the foot of Mount Affile. Here life for Benedict was probably not as silent as anticipated. Word spread far and wide of a miracle that had occurred: On one occasion a woman borrowed a ceramic wheat sieve from neighbors. It accidentally fell to the floor and smashed into pieces. Benedict, seeing her distress at breaking the sieve, took it aside and fell to his knees in prayer. When he had finished praying, the sieve was again whole as it had been before.

Finding that he was responding more and more to the apostolic injunction to forsake all to follow Christ, Benedict moved again, this time to a cave in Subiaco (*sacro speco*, "the holy cave"), east of Rome. At Subiaco he withdrew from society, deliberately choosing a life of solitude and hard work, and was visited only by the monk Romanus, who brought him food and other necessities.

Here again Benedict's desire to embrace the eremitic life was not to be fulfilled; before long he became known and again attracted a following of aspirants who elected him abbot of a local monastery. One day Benedict ordered that a brother be given a sickle to cut away the briars in a garden on the bank of a lake. While the man was cutting at the thick underbrush, the iron blade flew away from the handle and fell into the lake, where the water was too deep to permit the blade's recovery. When Benedict heard about this accident, he took the handle and struck it into the lake. Immediately the blade returned from the bottom of the lake and came back to the handle.

Benedict

Blest in name, more blest in calling,
    Benedict, still we sing your praise,
proud to be your sons and daughters,
    following in your proven ways.
From those days when by the mountain
    in the cave some way from Rome,
you were call'd to seek the Godhead
    and to live for God alone.

In that hidden cave new wisdom
    and new holiness were born,
till towards the light in darkness
    brothers came in search of dawn,
begging you to be their father
    and to guide them to that home
where the one who is eternal
    welcomes all who are his own.

Slow long years distilled your wisdom
    into the words that are your Rule,
that we too might learn to follow,
    learning to live in God's own school,
learn to love and learn to listen,
    learning with patience to obey,
how the humble find the Kingdom,
    how the grumblers lose the way.

Humbly following in your footsteps,
    Benedict, now we praise your name,
thanking God for your great wisdom
    letting our faithfulness proclaim
still the wonder of that vision
    of this world that you received:
all the beauty of creation
    in a sunbeam you perceived.

In the valleys, on the mountains,
    in the cities of our land,
still we pledge our lives in worship,
    building on God's own rock, not sand;
and in leading lives of silence,
    disciplined lives of work and prayer,
with great joy we prove by patience
    that our God is truly here.

Written by Fr. Ralph Wright, O.S.B., St. Louis Abbey, St. Louis, Mo.

The followers of Benedict in Subiaco, not all that accustomed to a life of discipline and virtue, soon discovered that they could not endure the rigors of the new regime that he proposed. Plotting together, they agreed to kill Benedict by poisoning his wine. However, when the moment came for the abbot to drink, he made the sign of the cross over the glass and it immediately broke into pieces, the drink of death being unable to endure Benedict's sign of life.

After his problems with the rebellious monks, Benedict returned to the eremitical life but was once again persuaded by the increasing pressure of those who felt they needed him to found not just one but, according to St. Gregory, twelve monasteries back at Subiaco. Benedict appointed an abbot for this, his first monastic foundation, and it continued to flourish after he himself left with some of his monks for Montecassino. Two monasteries still flourish there today, one on the cliff, built around the *sacro speco*, and the other, named for his sister Scholastica, in the valley.

Montecassino is located about eighty miles southeast of Rome. It was there that Benedict and his followers destroyed a pagan temple dedicated to Apollo and built his most famous monastery. During a period of about fifteen years, when Benedict served as abbot of Montecassino, he composed his influential Rule, which crystallized the best of the monastic tradition that he had absorbed during so many years of practice. Thoroughly imbued with intimate knowledge of the scriptures and the wisdom of the church fathers, Benedict reached a point near the end of his life when he glimpsed the glory of God. As St. Gregory tells in the *Second Book of the Dialogues*:

Benedict, the man of the Lord, having advanced the time for night prayers, was already at his vigils while the brothers were still asleep. He stood by the window praying to the Lord Almighty. All at once, in the middle of the night, he looked up and saw a light spreading from on high and completely repelling the darkness of the night. It shone with such splendor that it surpassed the light of the day, even though it was shining in the midst of darkness. A marvelous thing followed in this contemplation for, as he himself related afterwards, the whole world was brought before his eyes, gathered up, as it were, under a single ray of light.[1]

This ray of light was to illumine all of Benedictine learning during the dark periods of the Middle Ages and far beyond.

The Rule

The Rule was written by St. Benedict for his monks at Montecassino during the first part of the sixth century. In it we hear Benedict's voice teaching and admonishing the monks in his charge. There are no personal references made—Benedict's words are purely prescriptive—and yet one can certainly infer the character and virtue of the man who speaks so discretely and clearly.

Abbot Patrick Barry, O.S.B., to whose new translation of the Rule we constantly refer,[2] mentions in his preface that "the language of the Rule is rooted in a Latin version of the Old and New Testaments which was so familiar to Benedict that his writing, quite apart from the many direct quotations, constantly reflects and echoes the words of scripture." He adds, however, that it is "colloquial and non-literary," musical with "a strong

sense of rhythm and even of poetry."[3] The best manuscript existing today, Codex Sangallensis 914, dates from the early ninth
century and is found in St. Gall, Switzerland.[4]

In the Rule, Benedict reveals himself as a wise, holy, firm
paternal abbot able to combine strict principles with moderation
and humanity. He never prescribes any discipline that would be
excessive or beyond the capability of the average monk. The
monks have what they need—food, drink, lodging, materials for
study and work—and are not required to engage in the austere
measures that characterized much Eastern monasticism at the
time.

The values most emphasized by Benedict are those still
espoused today, following his example: *obedience*—". . . not to
serve their own will nor to give way to their own desires and
pleasures, but they submit in their way of life to the decisions
and instructions of another";[5] *silence*—"After all, it is written in
scripture that one who never stops talking cannot avoid falling
into sin";[6] and *humility*—"We can imagine that he has placed the
steps of the ladder, held in place by the sides which signify our
living body and soul, to invite us to climb on them. Paradoxi-
cally, to climb upwards will take us down to earth, but stepping
down will lift us towards heaven."[7]

Each monastery was completely autonomous, having no
connection with any other superior except the local bishop. The
lack of disciplinary sanctions imposed from without has served to
maintain abbatial authority and the independence of the individual monastery so characteristic of the Benedictine Order
throughout the centuries. Most important of all has been love of
and reverence for God, followed by care for and hospitality toward
one's neighbor. Each guest to the monastery is to be welcomed as
if he or she were Jesus himself.

The Rule of St. Benedict has been alive and well through more than fourteen centuries. It has never remained static, but has developed, grown, diversified, matured, and branched into new creativeness. Throughout its existence it has cast new images and been the spiritual source of new perspectives—spiritual, literary, musical, artistic—that its author could never have anticipated.

Abbot Patrick Barry likens the Rule to mature old wine able to recall not only the sun and the soil of the vineyard but also the long dark vigil in a cool cellar. He feels that to read it is to "recall its tradition, its history, its development, and the changes it has brought to human life, what it has done to the human heart through the ages, what the human heart has made of it and how it may touch the human heart today."[8]

One may legitimately ask why the Rule has such appeal to so many people today, since a number of Benedict's comments were directed to monks of the sixth century and no longer apply, even in a monastic context. Abbot Barry feels that, above all, people are drawn by the transcendent beauty to which the Rule is a guide. This beauty is Christ himself. Abbot Barry believes that "Christ is still the center of the Rule, attracting by his truth and goodness indeed, but most profoundly and universally by the irresistible beauty of his self-giving, which we call love."[9] It is this quality, shining through the Rule, that is so much needed in our time.

Pope St. Gregory the Great

In 590 Gregory, named "the Great," became the first of fifty followers of St. Benedict to occupy the papal throne. He is the primary source for our knowledge of St. Benedict and the person for whom the chant was named. History confirms the breadth of

Gregory's other accomplishments: theologian and interpreter of scripture, vigilant guardian of the church's doctrine, writer of an impressive correspondence, able administrator and friend of the poor, and authority most responsible for the spread of Benedictine monasticism to the British Isles.

Gregory was born in Rome in 540, seven years before the death of Benedict. He was the son of a Roman senator and belonged to a devoutly Christian family that had already produced two pontiffs. During his youth, the city of Rome was experiencing the catastrophic aftermath of its fall some seventy years before. As a replacement for the weak and decadent civilization of Rome there came wave after wave of brutal Germanic tribes streaming across Europe to storm the city's gates. The Lombards, who invaded northern Italy in 568 and established a kingdom in the Po valley, were crueler than any other. They burned Rome's churches, tore down and terrorized its monasteries, and left neighboring farmland ravaged and uninhabited.

After completing law studies in 573, Gregory accepted the call to become prefect of Rome, a position where he believed he could provide the citizens with a measure of safety and protection. This work he resigned, however, within a year, preferring to give himself to the monastic way of life. Disposing of all the trappings of his office, he began to devote himself to an existence of poverty, chastity, and obedience.

Gregory founded St. Andrew's Monastery in Rome, in sight of his own home, and remained there for several years that he later recalled as the happiest of his life. In 578 he was again pressed into public service when Pope Benedict I made him a deacon of Rome, quite against his will. Further responsibilities were added when he was sent to serve as permanent ambassador to the Byzantine court at Constantinople.

Meanwhile, Rome continued to be besieged, this time by floods that threatened to submerge the Italian peninsula. The River Tiber overflowed its banks and food supplies were totally destroyed. Pope Pelagius fell victim to the plague, leaving the church without a head and the people without a protector. It was at this moment of crisis that Gregory was elected pope.

In spite of the fact that Gregory was fifty years old, fatigued, and in ill health, he proved himself more than equal to the task. He organized the seven districts of the city and gave food, clothing, and shelter to the multitudes who had come to Rome seeking protection from the Lombards. He did much to assist the poor and homeless.

Adept at handling the pressing needs of the temporal kingdom, Gregory was also able to attend to the spiritual by giving his mind to the work at hand and keeping his heart fixed upon God. During his pontificate he wrote the *Regula Pastoralis* or *Pastoral Rule* on the duties of a bishop, which has long remained the textbook for clerical life, and *The Dialogues*, already mentioned. As protector of the liturgical life of the church, he fostered the development of the *Sacramentary*, a volume of prayers or collects said at Mass. There is also considerable evidence that he created the famous Roman *schola cantorum* (school of singers), but there is no doubt that he was very instrumental in the gathering and compilation of the liturgical chant.

In 597 Gregory sent Augustine, one of the monks from his own monastery of St. Andrew, accompanied by forty other monks, to convert England. One can imagine that they were carrying with them a copy of Benedict's Rule, but in a letter quoted by the Venerable Bede (672–735), historian and doctor of the church known particularly for his *Ecclesiastical History of the English People*, the monks were explicitly instructed that the example

of their monastic life should be the principal means for convert-
ing pagans. This was the first apostolic monastic mission, com-
missioned by the greatest of the popes. An important result was
that the metropolitan see (seat or center of authority) of Canterbury, founded by Augustine, became monastic, followed later by
eight other Benedictine monastic cathedrals (minsters) in England. Nothing like this happened in any other country in
Europe. Another consequence was that when, during the Reformation, the Anglican liturgy was developed, it turned out to be
in many respects derived from the Benedictine liturgy. It is also
said that Gregory encouraged the adoption of Benedictine
monasticism in Frankish and Lombard monasteries.

Gregory died on March 12, 604 at the age of sixty-four and
was immediately acclaimed a saint by the faithful. Because of the
depth and range of his thought and the heroic holiness of his
life, he became one of the church's four great doctors of the
patristic period, alongside Jerome, Ambrose, and Augustine.[10]

The Second Book of the Dialogues

Gregory's *Second Book of the Dialogues*, *The Life of St. Benedict*,
was certainly not a biography in the modern sense of the word.
Its purpose was to strengthen the faith of the monks by offering
them the example of a patron who had all the qualities of a man
of God, conquered the world's temptations, performed miracles,
and practiced monastic virtue to an eminent degree. Above all,
Gregory wanted to edify and inspire, to show that the saints of
God were still working within the church despite all the political and social chaos of the time. The *Second Book of the Dialogues*, though stylized and hagiographic, is historical as well.

Gregory takes great pains to give testimony from reliable sources and traditions. His information is gathered from people who are still living and concerns places well known to them.

To understand Gregory's *Dialogues* it may be well to remember that the medieval mind looked at the world symbolically. Events were not viewed as simple happenings. Reality did not and does not hang suspended in a vacuum as people throughout the ages have often believed. Physical or natural reality was seen as penetrated by supernatural reality, infused and charged with meaning so that whatever was seen became a sign. Also, the belief that the New Testament was a fulfillment of the Old led many to see symmetries and confirmations between the events of Jesus' life and those in the lives of the prophets or between his words and the sayings of the psalms.

The similarities of the style of life and set of beliefs of the early ascetics and monastics obviously led to similarities of experience, so that we should not be surprised to find this reflected in the accounts of their lives. This has led scholars to speculate that these parallels were due to literary "borrowings," often of little other than the form. But it must be remembered that the purpose of the composition was less anecdotal and historical than edificatory. Obviously the writer would avail himself of all the power of symbolism for instructing his audience in the faith. It is not surprising, therefore, to find in Gregory's account parallels with events in the lives of prophets and other saints such as Anthony, Pachomius, and other desert fathers.

In his perceptive study, *An Interpretation of the Second Dialogue of Gregory the Great*,[11] Pearce Cusack points to the fact that the first eight chapters of the *Second Dialogue* show many parallels between Benedict's eremitical existence at Subiaco and that of the Old Testament prophet Elijah living in the desert, while the remaining chapters concerning Benedict's cenobitic life at Monte-cassino resemble the story of Elijah's disciple, Elisha. The reason these two prophets were chosen by Gregory to illustrate the life of Benedict may lie mainly in the example of their ascetic lives— that they could forsake everything to follow God. Benedict was willing to do the same and therefore shared in their holiness.

The story can be considered a description of Benedict's spe-cific virtues and talents, though it may also appear as a confla-tion of the various gifts of a man of God in general. Like the apostles, Benedict worked with his hands; like Peter and Paul, he left all things to follow Christ.

Gregory wanted what he said about Benedict to carry a sym-bolic as well as a literal meaning. Cusack points out that this desire to reveal a deeper truth was consciously embedded in the structure of the *Second Dialogue,* in the way that numbers were used in its creation.

Medieval Numerology

In order to understand and also appreciate possible use of num-ber in the elaboration of the church's liturgy, let us look briefly at medieval numerology. In his article in the *Catholic Encyclo-pedia* on "Use of Numbers,"[12] Herbert Thurston points out that although the church fathers condemned the magical use of num-bers and denounced any system that rested upon an exclusively numerical basis, they "regarded the numbers of Holy Writ as full of mystical meanings, and they considered the interpreta-tion of these mystical meanings as an important branch of exe-gesis." Thurston emphasizes the powerful influence of numbers by saying:

There can be no doubt that, influenced mainly by Biblical precepts, but also in part by the prevalence of this
philosophy of numbers all around them, the Fathers
down to the time of Bede and even later gave much
attention to the sacredness and mystical significance
... of certain numerals.

He goes on to say that:

At a period, then, when the Church was forming her
liturgy and when Christian teachers so readily saw mystical meanings underlying everything which had to do
with numbers, it can hardly be doubted that a symbolical
purpose must constantly have guided the repetition of
acts and prayers in the ceremonial of the Holy Sacrifice
and indeed in all public worship.

And he concludes that:

We are justified, we say, in assigning some mystical
meaning to all those things, which may not perhaps
have been very closely conceived by those who instituted these ceremonies, but which nevertheless had an
influence in determining their choice of why the ceremony should be performed in this particular way and not
otherwise.

Gregory was no doubt aware of an understanding of numbers
dating at least as far back as Pythagoras, a Greek philosopher of
the sixth century B.C. According to this view, numbers had a

threefold aspect: one was physical, the practical application of counting; one was mental, the way to understand more abstract relationships in creation; and one was pure or divine. The pure or divine quality was the most interesting to the medieval mind, since the view of philosophers and writers was that the immaterial, the eternal, constitutes the true reality while that which is subject to formation and destruction (i.e., that which can be counted) is not actually real.

Rather than associating number with *quantity* and creating hierarchies of "having," the church fathers looked instead to the *quality* of numbers and their state of "being." *One* was the principle of all things, representing God. Everything emanated from it and it emanated from nothing. It was indivisible.

Two represented duality, the many polarities—light and darkness, right and wrong, man and woman, positive and negative—which made up their experience of the material world.

Three was to theologians the embracing synthesis, the Trinity of Father, Son, and Holy Spirit, the union of thought, word, and deed or the Way, the Truth, and the Life. Christ's Resurrection took place after three days in the tomb; his age at the time of his crucifixion was thirty-three.

Four was the number of the material world, standing for stability but also rigidity. It was concerned with the first known ways of ordering time into four seasons and space into four cardinal directions.

Five was the number for man incarnate with his five senses —hearing, touch, sight, taste, and smell; his head and four limbs; the five fingers of each hand and the five toes of each foot.

Six was the first so-called perfect number of the created world, being both the sum and the product of its factors ($1 + 2 + 3 = 6$

and 1 x 2 x 3 = 6). The cube, composed of six squares, was the ideal form for any closed construction. The Star of David, with its six points made up of two superimposed triangles, was the symbol of harmonious union.

Most mysterious of all was the sacred number *seven*, representing the joining of the body of the earth, i.e., its four elements of air, fire, water, and earth, its four cardinal directions in space, its four seasons, with the world of spirit, i.e., the three persons of the Holy Trinity. It is the perfect number, composed of the sum of the first divisible whole number, four, and the first indivisible, three. It is no coincidence, therefore, that seven is so extensively used in Christian religious symbolism—the seven sacraments, the seven gifts of the Holy Spirit.

Eight, the number used by Benedict in the Opus Dei and probably by the early Christian liturgists in the development of worship throughout the Christian year, was said to be particularly auspicious. If all events of importance were seen to take place in seven steps, as will be explained later, then eight marked their successful conclusion and at the same time the beginning of a new cycle on a level higher than the first. It is the number associated with Christian baptism—whence the octagonal form of the baptistery—but also with the final resurrection, the beginning of new and unending life with God.

The early theologians saw *nine* as the highest, fullest number within the decade, bringing human gestation to completion and having its root in the number three. *Ten* marked the beginning of another decade and was considered to have all the qualities of the one. It represents the unity of diversity.

Herbert Thurston, in his article "Symbolism"[13] appearing in the *Catholic Encyclopedia*, speaks of the *Rationale divinorum offi-*

ciorum of Durandus, wherein every detail of the construction of a medieval church is shown to have special symbolic significance. In this the mystical interpretation of numbers is very important. Thurston says that "three is the number figuring the divine nature, four, the number of the material world, and twelve, the penetration of matter with spirit." Twelve was therefore the number of the universal church of which the apostles were the symbol: twelve persons carrying knowledge of the Divine Trinity to the four corners of the world. Thurston continues by saying that "eight denotes perfection and completion, for the visible world was made in seven days and the invisible kingdom of grace follows upon that."

Thurston concludes by stating that "there can be little doubt that much of this symbolism of numbers is to be traced back to Egypt and Assyria, where the movements of the seven planets, as men then counted them, were continuously studied and where the elements of three and four into which seven was divided lent themselves to other combinations also regarded as peculiarly sacred, for example the number sixty, the product of three, four, and five."

The jubilee year, or the completion of a fifty-year cycle, is described in the twenty-fifth chapter of Leviticus. God told Moses to instruct the Israelites to "count off seven weeks of years, seven times seven years, so that the period of seven weeks of years gives forty-nine years . . . and you shall hallow the fiftieth year and you shall proclaim liberty throughout the land to all its inhabitants. It shall be a jubilee for you . . ." (Lev 25:8 and 25:10). Fifty represented completion, happiness, rest, the return of property to its rightful owners, the forgiveness of debt, the freeing of slaves.

Gregory's Use of Number

Clearly the symbolic and qualitative meaning of numbers does not escape Gregory when he speaks about Benedict's early disciples and how they were organized in *twelve* monasteries with an abbot and *twelve* monks in each. Benedict spent *three* years in seclusion at Subiaco; *three* stones marked the spot where God, in answer to Benedict's prayer, caused water to rush forth from a mountain previously dry; Benedict's sister Scholastica died *three* days after visiting him. The *Second Book of the Dialogues* is replete with specific references to numbers, but even more fascinating is the way in which they figure in the work as a whole. According to the analysis of Pearce Cusack, the *Vita* is made up of two main parts: eight chapters, the number for one complete cycle, are devoted to Benedict's life at Subiaco and the remaining chapters deal with his experience at Montecassino. If one looks closely at the specific exempla or episodes, one can see that they follow a very specific pattern of 5 + 5 + 5 + 5 + 12 + 12 + 5:

    5 examples of his life as a hermit
    5 examples of when he was abbot of the first monastery
    5 examples of his problems with followers
    5 examples of his struggles with demons
   12 prophecies he made
   12 miracles he performed
    5 visions he had at the end of his life.

Added to the twenty-five examples of worldly episodes and guiding visions were twelve chapters of prophecy and twelve of miracles, making a jubilee number of forty-nine episodes which, symbolically, would gain for Benedict the joy and peace of heaven.

Laeta quies magni ducis

Today we recollect and with great joy
the quiet passing of a mighty leader—
a recollection bringing gifts of light.

To those of humble heart new grace is given;
as things both new and old are called to mind
they echo music in the honest soul.

Let our hearts then swell with wonder
as we watch him like a patriarch
climb the pathway of the rising sun.

When we see the number of his seed
Abraham our Father comes to mind—
the greater among lesser stars perceived.

See, a raven meets his every need
in this little cave and we recall
Elijah, the great patriarch of old.

Elisha's wonders from those far off times
are echoed as he rescues from the lake
the blade that left the sickle's handle.

His purity resembles that of Joseph,
his prophecy brings Jacob to our minds—
gifted with his visions in the night.

May he remember all his sons and daughters,
his family without number down the ages,
and know with them the joy of Christ for ever.
Amen. Alleluia.

Laeta quies magni ducis, Dona ferens novae lucis, Hodie recolitur. Charis datur piae menti, Corde sonet in ardenti Quidquid foris promitur. Hunc per callem Orientis Admiremur ascendentis Patriarchae speciem. Amplum semen magnae prolis Illum fecit instar solis, Abrahae persimilem. Corvum cernis ministrantem, Hinc Eliam latitantem Specu nosce parvulo. Elisaeus dignoscatur, Cum securis revocatur De torrentis alveo. Illum Joseph candor morum. Illum Jacob futurorum Mens effecit conscia. Ipse memor suae gentis, Nos perducat in manentis Semper Christi gaudia. Amen. Alleluia.

*Sequence for the Passing of St. Benedict, monastic liturgy of March 21,
translated by Fr. Ralph Wright, O.S.B., St. Louis Abbey, St. Louis , Mo.*

Gregory's portrait of Benedict is that of a person who brings together the strength and discipline of the desert fathers, the cosmic vision of the prophets, and the miraculous healing power of the apostles and Christ himself. Few have been so honored by a disciple!

Benedictinism through Time

Now that we have laid the historical foundation by giving background about St. Benedict, Pope St. Gregory the Great, and the qualitative and symbolic importance of numbers in the medieval mind-set, we need to spend a little time with Benedictinism, the practice of monastic life that is the direct outgrowth of the clear, flexible directives written by St. Benedict into his Rule and lived out by his monastic communities. Over the centuries this consecrated way of life has retained the basic nature set forth by its founder. It has remained essentially traditional in its outlook while, at the same time, opening its arms to welcome creative and innovative change. Here we will briefly outline the spirit and way of life of the Benedictines, the context into which we will place all of the musical considerations to follow.

Benedictine Vows

Persons who choose the Benedictine monastic way of life make three vows that have remained the same for nearly fourteen hundred years, ever since they were enunciated by St. Benedict in the early sixth century. These are *obedience*, *conversion of life*, and *stability*. Benedictines see obedience—to others in the community; to their lawfully elected superiors; to the reality of life; to God—as liberating and not in any way a denigration of self. The abbot or abbess in charge of the monastery or convent is also under discipline to follow the rule of the community and to make every attempt to guide, following the example set by Christ. The monks or nuns should readily and willingly listen and accept spiritual counsel both from their leaders and from other members of the community. As Fr. Demetrius Dumm, O.S.B., points out in his insightful book, *Cherish Christ Above All,* "It is so much easier to live in the illusion of the importance of one's own projects than to have another evaluate them in terms of their usefulness for the benefit of all."[14] This steady chipping away of personal arrogance and its replacement with a sense of humility—honesty about oneself and recognition of one's own place in the community and the world—has had the effect over the centuries of freeing Benedictines to make great contributions to religion and culture.

The word "obedience" comes from the Latin *ob audire,* "from, or out of listening," and in this context means listening to the inner promptings of Spirit known in the heart. St. Benedict considers listening so important that he begins his Rule with these words:

> Listen, child of God, to the guidance of your teacher. Attend to the message you hear and make sure that it pierces to your heart, so that you may accept with willing freedom and fulfill by the way you live the directions that come from your loving Father.[15]

For the Benedictines, then, obedience is never to be compared to obedience exacted in the civil realm, where people are often forced into subjection to the will of others. Here the motive is "out of love of God" alone. Above all else, obedience is concerned with the intimate personal and community discernment of the will of God and the following of Christ's example of obedience to the Father.

Conversion of life as viewed by the monks of Benedict's time was the promise to observe the full monastic regimen as it was practiced in a particular monastery and defined by a particular rule. Today this promise continues to mean that Benedictines will abandon the secular way of life and accept the way of life of the monastery where they live.

The vow of stability adds that the monks or nuns will be committed to staying in one place, where others will come to know them. This will enable them to learn both the good and the painful about themselves. Rather than leaving the community as soon as the truth begins to hurt, they remain there in order to be shaped and formed. Benedict himself had little patience with flightiness. In speaking of the *gyrovagues* (Latin *gyrus* from Greek *guros*, "circle" and Latin *vagus* "wandering"; literally, a monk who walks in circles) he said, "They are always on the move; they never settle to put down the roots of stability; it is their own wills that they serve or seek the satisfaction of their own gross appetites."[16]

While this has never been interpreted as a criticism of monks who, for legitimate purpose, are obliged to move around, it serves as a powerful reminder of the Benedictines' inner, spiritual commitment to one community located in a specific place. Stability also includes the idea that Benedictines, without compromising their basic way of life, will be sensitive to the needs of the local community and its people. The Benedictine presence will be felt but will not intrude.

The Benedictine Way

Humility, one of the essential characteristics of the Benedictine way of life, is often viewed in modern life as a sort of negative asceticism, difficult to accept as something desirable or even beautiful. More valued are assertive, competitive qualities designed to take one to the top. Abbot Patrick Barry,[17] tongue in cheek, wonders what life would be like if our education and acculturation succeeded in making us all winners, all leaders, everybody up there on top! He is reminded of the head of an Oxford college who accepted a student with—according to school reports—no gift for leadership. In accepting him, this director wrote that, since his other candidates all seemed to be outstanding leaders, it would be nice to have at least one student who knew how to follow!

Abbot Barry points out that the quality of humility is no fad of monasticism but lies deep in gospel teaching, a mandate for all of Christ's followers. Humility is seen as the appropriate response of a human being placed in a universe where all ambition, pride of achievement, will to dominate, or thirst for power may be snuffed out in an instant. We are frail and vulnerable creatures, "hanging," as Abbot Barry puts it "in utter dependence on the Creator in every fiber of our being—in every fancy of our mind, in every hope, and in every fear."[18]

Humility is inspired by total awe and reverence for the Creator but also by the model of Christ himself, who, in following the will of God, "made himself obedient unto death." Seen in this way, humility becomes an extension of monastic obedience. The monk or nun does not seek to indulge his or her own desires but, rather, to follow God's will.

Silence is the norm in Benedictine monasteries; speech or any other noise is considered the exception rather than the rule. This silence is sought out and loved. Monks and nuns see it as the ambiance needed for facing self and God, the pre-condition for prayer, reflection, reading, and living with awareness of the divine presence. Outside the monastery walls, this love of silence is often viewed as something strange, even fearful. Modern life has created a lifestyle that is almost never free of persistent din and activity.

Abbot Barry cites the example[19] of a group of Catholic youth in the United States who went to study camps in log cabins in the woods—lodgings supplied with all the modern conveniences that teenagers expect and feel they need. One day the organizers decided to give the participants an experience of being utterly silent and alone. They took them singly to safe places in the forest—no one to talk to, no sound but nature's, not even the companionship of their beloved Walkmans. The teenagers had to wait for half an hour before being rescued. Some of them broke down and, terrified, cried for help after five minutes. Those who lasted half an hour fell weeping into their rescuers' arms. They had never before experienced silence and could not endure finding themselves deprived of the incessant stream of sound with which they normally lived.

This pollution of the environment through excessive noise—constant verbal chatter, blasting music, uncontrolled barking of dogs, deafening roar of leaf blowers, and honking of cars—often goes on unnoticed; people simply learn to "tune it out" in an effort of adaptation for survival. To this predicament the Benedictines offer the option of elected quiet, where they themselves, and the visitors to their guesthouses, may rediscover the gifts of silence and put aside all of this agitation.

Lectio Divina *and Chant*

A very important part of Benedictine life is study of the Holy Scriptures (Christian Bible) and the writings of the early church fathers or spiritual teachers. Called *lectio divina* or divine reading, it is not reading for information in the ordinary sense. Rather, it is a more reflective endeavor wherein the reader is *in-formed* or inwardly moved by what is read. In Benedict's time it was said to be a slow, deliberate, and meditative murmuring of the sacred text, with pauses to allow for prayerful response. Demetrius Dumm, O.S.B., describes it in this way:

> The most notable feature of this method was its strong emphasis on the *spiritual* sense of scripture, that is, on a meaning that benefited from the light of faith and which, therefore, transcended the literal or obvious meaning. Such a methodology began with the assumption that the Bible was the word of God and that, as such, it could have meanings that were quite possibly unknown to its human author.[20]

The purpose of the reading was, and still is, to establish a connection between the reading and the life experience of the reader.

Lectio divina begins with a careful reading of a text, usually the Bible or a commentary upon it. Today this is usually practiced silently. The purpose is first to understand the text on an immediate and obvious level. It may mean looking up words in the dictionary or other sources. Once this has been accomplished, the practitioner moves on, in a second step, to pondering the text, seeking meaning that applies to him or her at that very moment of practice. Certain words or phrases may have particular meaning, or may help the individual to recall life experiences or things that have already been learned. The third step is a response in the form of short prayers that express the individual's heart-felt reaction to what has been discovered in the text. The fourth and final step of *lectio* is contemplation, said to be a gift of the Holy Spirit. Here the individual's consciousness may move beyond the text to an experience of deep communion with God.

This method of *lectio divina* is often used by Benedictines when they approach any kind of learning. First, the material is carefully studied and its relationship to Christian teachings evaluated in an effort to penetrate the symbolic as well as the purely literal meanings. Gratitude for what has been learned and appreciated will come about naturally and may be offered as a prayer of thanksgiving. Further contemplation will remind the monk or nun that the object of study is not an end in itself, but is a means toward a more profound understanding that will transcend benefits attained by superficial reading alone.

Qualities of Monastic Life

Fr. Jeremy Driscoll, O.S.B., writing on "Monastic Culture and the Catholic Intellectual Tradition,"[21] provides a very clear description of the face that Benedictinism presents to the world. He speaks of the tension that is inevitably created between the monastery and the mores of the prevailing culture. In modern society, time is measured in minutes and divided into seconds, whereas for monastics the century might be a more appropriate measure! The slow rhythm of the monastery, which allows for the expression of qualitative differences, contrasts with the outside world's desire to accomplish much in a short time, to have instant access to vast amounts of information, to be impatient with whatever takes time to mature.

Benedictines are aware of the importance of words (for example, the name of their founder, "Benedict," means "the man of good speech"). In the practice of *lectio*, a single word can be savored and all its symbolism and multi-layered nuances drawn forth. Contrast this with our society, where words are often too numerous and sometimes create a screen that actually prevents rather than encourages communication.

Benedictine monks and nuns pledge themselves to a life of sexual chastity that is dramatically opposed to the liberal sexual mores found in the modern world. Emphasis is placed on the creation of real community, where monastics live together with profound respect and courtesy. This idea has been well expressed by the lay Benedictines of the Manquehue Movement[22] in Chile in their Little Rule:

> The brethren themselves are to show warmth to each other and also towards all others with whom they come into contact. It is just as St. Paul said: "Accept one another, then, for the sake of God's glory, as Christ accepted you" (Romans 15:7). To offer such a welcome to another means to recognize and adore Christ himself in that person, to open one's heart to the love of that other person, to make space in one's thinking and listen to another among all the preoccupations and tasks that absorb the mind, to make every effort to meet others' needs from one's own resources whatever their requirements—whether material or spiritual.[23]

In the measure that spiritual people are able to find Christ within, their capacity for reaching outward to others in his name is increased. Simply put, the Benedictine becomes hospitable to Christ's presence in his or her own life and is therefore ready to acknowledge and welcome it in others. As Abbot Rooney has stated:

> We try to love one another in community in response to the God who has first loved us all, enough to have Jesus die for us … We care for each other, whether we are young or old, accepting each other's foibles and weak- nesses for what they are. St. Paul said, "We bear the treasure (i.e., Divine Life) in clay pots." As a result of that love, we welcome guests, especially the tired and wounded in spirit, so that they can find healing in the midst of the serenity and regular rhythm of a healthy human life that is focused in God.[24]

In the Benedictine ethos, moderation in all things is very important. Monks and nuns are asked to give up personal owner- ship of and claim on the material things that they use, but the abbot or abbess sees that each one has everything needed in appropriate measure, not too much but not too little. Benedict makes it very clear in his Rule that he is not proposing a way of life that is too difficult or too extreme for anyone who is suffi- ciently motivated to follow.

The Benedictine motto *"ora et labora"* ("pray and work") indicates that, in addition to prayer and study, physical work is a vital part of life. The way that the task is done places value on compassion as well as efficiency. Every tool is cared for as if it were a sacred vessel of the altar. Every item or talent used is perceived as holy in the sight of God. As a result, Benedictines are exemplary in ecological awareness and in stewardship of the gifts of the earth.

That the Benedictine way of life has more than just passing appeal can be seen in the large numbers of persons who are now regularly seeking refreshment and renewal through participation in monastic retreats.[25] In the new millennium we may anticipate an even greater number of lay movements and communities looking to Benedictinism for inspiration. Many of these world-wide lay movements go even further by using the Rule of St. Benedict in developing what is now called and officially recognized by the church as "consecrated lay life." Fruitful ecumenical relationships have also been established between Benedictine Catholics and Lutheran and Episcopal faith communities who follow the Rule.

Benedict felt that the kingdom of God is closer when people who come from very diverse backgrounds live together in peace and love. The focus of the Benedictines on the awareness of the presence of God in and through all the complexities of life, their practice of holiness, and their love of wisdom manifest in a variety of very practical endeavors, many of which have to do with the education of the young. Their hallmark is care and attention to the work so that it, in turn, may reflect back, literally or symbolically, some of the radiance of God.

3
The Opus Dei
and the Liturgical Year

"Make prayer the first step."
St. Benedict

The Opus Dei

From the earliest years following Christ's life on earth, those who were baptized "devoted themselves to the apostles' teaching and fellowship, to the breaking of bread and the prayers."[1] It is believed that individual Christians first prayed alone or within their families. However, as time went on and persecution of believers lessened, it became customary to designate special times for communal or group prayer. Often selected was the last hour of the day, when light changed to darkness and the lamps were lighted, or the first hour of the day, when the daystar arose. Other periods of the day, often beginning at the third, sixth, and ninth hours (roughly 9 A.M., noon, and 3 P.M.) were also sanctified in this way. Christians saw this coming together for prayer as a necessary complement to the eucharistic meal instituted by

Christ, a means by which its grace could overflow into the whole day, blessing and consecrating each of its activities.

For the early desert fathers and mothers, prayer referred to the unceasing prayer of the heart; it was unstructured and ongoing. By the time of St. Benedict's Rule, however, there were well established patterns of worship prescribed for the monastic community as a whole. Benedict specifically states that "[God's] presence to us is never so strong as while we are celebrating the work of God in the oratory."[2]

Further on in the Rule, Benedict speaks of the scriptural injunction found in the psalms regarding these periods of prayer and praise to be carried out during the day and even in the night:

> The words of the Psalm are: I have uttered your praises seven times during the day.[3] We shall fulfill that sacred number of seven if at the time of Lauds, Prime, Terce, Sext, None, Vespers, and Compline we perform the duty of our service to God, because it was of these day hours that the Psalm said: I have uttered your praise seven times during the day. About the night vigil that same Psalm says: In the middle of the night I arose to praise you.[4] And so at these times let us offer praise to our Creator because of his justice revealed in his judgments[5]— that is at Lauds, Prime, Terce, Sext, None, Vespers and Compline and in the night let us arise to praise him.[6]

The plan was arranged so that across the whole day and night there would be a continuous remembering of Christ, a way to return to contemplation if the monks' attention had temporarily strayed due to the world's demands. This is variously called "Opus Dei" ("work of God"), the "Divine Office" (Latin *officium*, "performance of a duty"), or the "Liturgical Hours." It is important to note that "Hours" here refer to periods during the day given over to prayer. They were actually observed at the *temporal* hours which, themselves, varied in length according to the season. The Roman reckoning of daytime, which Benedict used, started with sunrise, called the "first hour" *(prima hora)* and extended to "twelfth hour" *(duodecima hora)* that occurred at sunset. The intervening temporal hours were arranged accordingly so that in summer, when days were longer, there was a more extended period of time allotted to each of the hours. In winter this interval was shorter. The twelve nighttime hours, which began at sunset and ended at sunrise, were seasonally shortened or lengthened as well.

So complicated was the task of determining the proper time for the Opus Dei that it often became the abbot's responsibility. One practical solution was for him to create a vertical sundial on the south-facing wall of the oratory or church—basically a hole intersected by a stick whose shadow would indicate the passing hours. (The direction of the movement of that shadow is still to be observed in the clockwise direction of our present-day clocks.) Most probably, with so much practice, it became simply a matter of the abbot's watching the sun directly, if there were a sun to be seen! This need to observe the Opus Dei on cloudy days may help to explain the interest of the medieval church in the building of mechanical clocks, such as the one erected in the 1300s at the cathedral of Rouen and still working today.

Although the Rule is the earliest document to contain all eight liturgical hours, Benedict is normally credited only with the establishment of Compline (Latin *hora completa*, "final hour"), the prayer sung before retiring at night. The other hours had developed gradually during the first six centuries of the Christian era. The first was the night office, Vigils (Latin *vigilia*, "wakefulness"), originally keeping watch on the night before Easter in anticipation of Christ's Resurrection. This was then observed weekly, before each Sunday, and eventually it was divided into three separate prayer hours—Vespers (Latin *vespera*, "evening") at sunset, Matins (Latin *matutinus*, "of the morning"), at about two in the morning, and Lauds (Latin *laud*, "praise"), at sunrise.

The liturgical hours of Prime, Terce, Sext, and None, named for the Roman first, third, sixth, and ninth hours, were gradually added. They are referred to as the "Lesser Hours" because they contain fewer psalms and last for a relatively short period of time.

Modern monasteries, influenced to some extent by the demands of temporal time, do not usually sing all the Lesser Hours but often schedule the Divine Office at sunrise (calling it Lauds), midday, late afternoon (Vespers), and early evening (Compline), sometimes adding an hour in the night for the monastic community alone.

The Music of the Opus Dei

Following Jewish tradition, and certainly that of other ancient civilizations, prayers and scriptural texts were given additional prominence by being intoned, often on one note. The rhythm was free, governed more by the natural accent and flow of speech than by imposed patterns.

In the earliest days, the Office was limited to chanting the psalms, the Christians' most important musical legacy from Judaism. By the fourth or fifth centuries, the liturgy was regulated and psalms were assigned to every hour of the Office in numbers varying from as few as three during the Lesser Hours to as many as eighteen during the night Vigil. Very often the psalms were connected with an antiphon (late Latin *antiphona*, "singing in response" or "singing against") or short scriptural texts sung before and after each psalm or, at the Lesser Hours, after an entire group of psalms. The basic pattern for chanting the hours consisted first of the antiphon, which had its own distinctive, freely composed melody, followed by the psalm, intoned largely on a single note but showing variations at the grammatical divisions of the text. The repeated antiphon then closed the sequence.

The one hundred and fifty psalms sung each week were united with only eight tones or recitation formulas, while the many hundreds of antiphons were all somewhat different melodies. Although the antiphons of any particular mode were very likely to show some of the same melodic sequences, the anonymous composers revealed their skill in the extraordinary variety of combinations they created. It is one of the most remarkable features of the Roman Catholic liturgy that, even to this day, each one of these short texts retains a melody different from any other.

The following example is an antiphon in honor of the feast of St. Anselm, for whom the primatial abbey is named. It is sung at morning prayer each day of the year by the monks at the abbey. Here it is printed in medieval square neumes as reconstructed at the Benedictine Abbey of Solesmes, France, in their *Antiphonale Monasticum* (Book of Monastic Antiphons):[7]

EXAMPLE 1: THE ANTIPHON "AD BENEDICTUS"

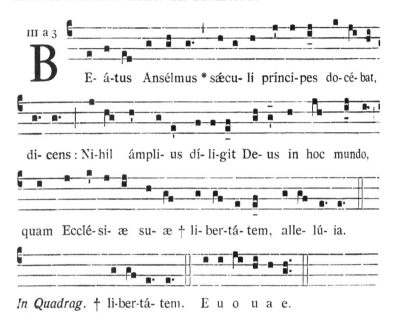

In Quadrag. † li-ber-tá- tem.   E u o   u a e.

Blessed Anselm taught the leaders of this world saying: "God loves nothing greater in this world than the freedom of his Church, alleluia."

From the *Antiphonale Monasticum*, Benedictines of Solesmes, eds. (Tournai, Belgium: Desclée & Co., 1934), 872. Permission granted by les Editions de Solesmes, Abbaye Saint-Pierre de Solesmes, Sablé-sur-Sarthe, France.

Before Benedict's time a number of sung scriptural texts or canticles were added to the psalms. At Lauds it was the *Benedictus Dominus Deus Israel*, "Blessed be the Lord God of Israel" (Luke 1:68–79). This song of Zechariah is sung at the moment of his son's circumcision, on the eighth day after his birth. It was then that Zechariah said, "His name is John" and his tongue was loosed and he sang these words in praise of God. At Vespers it was the Canticle of Mary, *Magnificat anima mea Dominum*, "My soul doth magnify the Lord" (Luke 1:46–55), said by the Holy Virgin in the presence of her cousin Elizabeth after the angel Gabriel had announced that she would give birth to the Christ Child. The canticle of Simeon, *Nunc dimittis servum tuum*, "Lord, let now thy servant depart in peace" (Luke 22:29–32), spoken by the elderly Simeon when he had seen Jesus, was sung at Compline in the churches but it was not part of the monastic observance until much later.

In addition to the singing of psalms and canticles with antiphons, there were lessons and short chapters or phrases read from scripture and followed by sung responsories.

The prescriptions in Benedict's Rule indicate that he included hymns in his Opus Dei. The psalms had a structure that lent itself very well to responsorial singing due to the division in half of most of their lines:

I will praise thee, O Lord, with my whole heart;
    I will show forth all thy marvelous works.
I will be glad and rejoice in thee;
    I will sing praise to thy name, O thou Most High.
                                        —Psalm 9:1–2

Hymns, on the other hand, were generally sung all the way through by everyone together. They were simple melodies divided into short stanzas or strophes, all of which had the same number of lines, the same metrical pattern, and the same rhyme scheme, if rhyme were present. The following example is taken from a Vesper Hymn for the First Sunday of Advent and dates from the third century:[8]

EXAMPLE 2: THE HYMN "CONDITOR ALME SIDERUM"

O gracious maker of the stars that curb the darkness of the night, to you we raise our humble prayers and trust in your redeeming light.

For in your mercy grieved to see our world so torn by sin and death, you came on earth to touch our wounds and heal us with your living breath.[9]

From the *Liber Cantualis*, Benedictines of Solesmes, eds. (Tournai, Belgium: Desclée & Co., 1978), 81–82. Permission granted by les Editions de Solesmes, Abbaye Saint-Pierre de Solesmes, Sablé-sur-Sarthe, France.

Many hymns never seem to have been associated with a particular melody and some of them were sung to well-known secular tunes. It is for this reason that the church wavered somewhat between approval and disapproval of their use. It is certain, however, that Ambrose, bishop of Milan from 374 to 397, personally wrote words for many melodies and gave particular importance to this form of congregational singing.[10]

The Divine Office Today

Throughout the centuries from the time of Benedict to the present, Benedictine nuns and monks have chanted the Divine Office, either as prescribed by their founder or, since the Second Vatican Council, on a revised schedule more easily related to the circumstances of contemporary life. The Liturgy of the Hours is no longer the prayer uniquely of the clergy and religious. It is now intended to be, as it was in the early church, the prayer of all, accessible to all, and possessed and understood by all.

This prayer of the church is continuous and is offered throughout the world for all humanity. It is therefore never a private individual devotion, even when it is said or sung by a person alone. Even a private recitation is seen to be participation in a public, ongoing act of worship of the whole church. From this perspective, Christ's words about his abiding presence "when two or three are gathered together in my name"[11] express a reality perfectly realized in this communal prayer. The distribution of the hours is intended to orient not only monks and nuns but all of God's people toward the Father, through Christ, and in the Spirit. Prayer in community is the guarantee of unity and charity among the members of the worshiping body. It also introduces a measure of objectivity into an individual's prayer life, lest he or she be inclined to emphasize only those aspects that appeal personally at any given moment.

Individual prayer might be compared to trying to fill a sieve by pouring cups of water into it. The water barely appears at the bottom and then is gone. Rather, one should take the sieve and throw it far out into the sea. There it becomes full of water and remains so. In worship one should not ladle little cupfuls of divine life into one's own individuality, but rather throw the individuality far out into the sea of divine life, which is Christ.

Spiritual life, if it is to be fruitful, demands a framework and consistency. Those who, like the monks and nuns, pray at the same time each day are the ones who continue the practice. Others often lose their resolve. The prayer of the church draws one into a powerful sense of the community of saints. These are the faithful people of God who across the centuries have consciously chosen, like Benedict and his followers, to join Christ in offering continuing gifts of praise and thanksgiving to the Lord of all. In the words of the Second Vatican Council,

> Christ Jesus, high priest of the new and eternal covenant, taking human nature, introduced into this earthly exile that hymn which is sung throughout all ages in the halls of heaven. He joins the entire community of mankind to Himself, associating it with His own singing of this canticle of divine praise. For He continues His priestly work through the agency of His Church, which is ceaselessly engaged in praising the Lord and interceding for the salvation of the whole world.[12]

The Octave as a Musical Model

Although verities of the faith are the same throughout the ages, the world in which they are proclaimed does change. For acceptance, their expression must rely on the common world view, on the images and stories shared by their audiences; therefore it is helpful to become acquainted with the views and images often taken for granted by authors, artists, or leaders of an era and which, consciously or not, shape their work.

Today's dominant world view, which subtly penetrates almost all thinking and influences societal values, may be said to be empirical, with physics and its mathematical framework as the model. Traditional civilizations, however, used music as an analogy of the order to be found in creation and in the world.[13] Our language is strewn with the remnants of once meaningful images, now barely poetic clichés, such as "the harmony of the spheres," "the symphony of life," and so on.

A frequently encountered pattern serving to structure events or large ensembles is the octave, which is a model recognizable as *"Do, Re, Mi, Fa, Sol, La, Si (Ti), Do."* It has been associated with wisdom schools through the ages, from the Egyptians, the Greeks, and the Romans down to such institutions as the Florentine Academy of Marsilio Ficino and Lorenzo de' Medici in the fifteenth century.

One may suspect that early Christian liturgists, like many early writers, were aware of and used, either consciously or subconsciously, numerical and musical concepts to organize their compositions and that the musical octave may have served as a guide in structuring the Opus Dei, the liturgical year, and the Mass. As we have already explained, the number seven, representing the joining by addition of the earthly four and the heavenly three, was considered to be the most sacred number after one and three. If each individual step in an important event were viewed as a musical note, the octave could become a metaphor for a series of steps which, like the musical octave, would form a cycle and offer a closure, allowing for a new series or octave to begin. From this viewpoint, then, any significant event could be seen as taking place in seven steps. The eighth step would signal the successful completion of one cycle or octave and the beginning of another. If the seven steps were consciously realized and proper energy were to be introduced at critical points, disorder and the tendency to stray in one's attention and resolve could be minimized.

Boris Mouravieff, who placed himself in the Russian Orthodox tradition, believed that the octave could be taken as a useful framework or model to make sense of the unfolding of significant activities that form a whole.[14] This evolution would take place in seven steps and move in a certain direction, determined by the initial plan or desire. However, he noted, unless certain specific conscious impulses were added along the way, there would always be a strong tendency to go astray or deviate from the original plan. (We can see this when we go shopping for gloves and end up with a coat!) In order that movement toward a specific goal take place without this deviation, complementary actions and extra effort needed to be introduced at precisely determined points.

The musical octave, whose seven steps were determined by Pythagoras through division of the vibrating string of a monochord, provided an experiential model whose power could be appreciated by listening. For those unfamiliar with singing the octave, it is important to note that not all the intervals between the notes are the same. The intervals between *Mi* and *Fa* and between *Si* and *Do* are half as large as the others:

Do	Re	Mi	Fa	Sol	La	Si	Do
WHOLE STEP	WHOLE STEP	HALF STEP	WHOLE STEP	WHOLE STEP	WHOLE STEP	HALF STEP	

In other words, if one sings two whole steps, *Do* to *Re* and *Re* to *Mi*, and then fails to rein in the energy to make the step between *Mi* and *Fa* only half as large, the octave goes entirely off course. For those familiar with the piano, it would be like playing C, D, E, F# instead of C, D, E, F. The same applies at the top of the octave, when after the whole steps *Fa* to *Sol*, *Sol* to *La*, and *La* to *Si*, there is again a special half-step requiring added attention. Mouravieff explained that, in an actual endeavor, the special effort required to pass the first interval between activities symbolically represented by *Mi* and *Fa* is provided by the human being, whereas the second interval between the events symbolized by *Si* and its completion in *Do* occurs through grace alone.

It is particularly important to note not only the placement of the intervals but also the fact that each note of the octave, *when sung in sequence*, takes on its own particular quality. Discover this by singing the octave on page 65 from bottom to top.

In order to understand the meaning of the octave model and its application to our own lives and then perhaps to appreciate its relevance in liturgy and in spiritual development, we will consider the effect, in experience, of moving from one of its steps to the next.

At the beginning of the octave, the *Do*, the whole activity is there in potential, having yet to be realized. We are aware of the goal or completed event that we have in mind and certain tools stand at our disposal—our belief system, our level of experience, our disposition toward the work, the means by which it can be achieved.

With the note *Re*, whether we are beginning a new job, writing a book, raising a child, or attending upon God in worship, there is some sort of challenge, something that disturbs the

---

THE OCTAVE

Do The conclusion and beginning of a new cycle.
      Interval—*also requires full attention and, through grace, leads to the perfect octave*

Si A note with tremendous tension, leaning toward the top *Do*.

La A more subdued note. The upward direction is strong but there is a quality of resignation.

Sol A bright, triumphant note

Fa A somewhat poignant note; it may return to whence it came or climb higher.
      Interval—*filled by human effort and increased attention.*

Mi A pleasant note, often used in later music for harmonizing

Re A first, tentative step that may easily lose resolve and return to *Do*

Do A strong initial impulse

---

status quo and propels us forward. We can perceive that movement and change are required.

The note *Mi* represents the feeling of stimulation and encouragement arising out of our firm decision to go ahead. We gather materials, study, seek information from others, and become fully and pleasantly engaged in the project.

It is, however, just as we are moving on from this pleasant and joyful step that some form of resistance is likely to occur. The more serious we are about whatever it is we are trying to accomplish, the more this difficulty comes up. At this point we can refuse to become engaged, turn aside from the lesson, and return to the comfortably familiar, or we can forge ahead. In a sense it is a crisis of commitment or faith. As the Chinese represent this word, it is both a "danger" and an "opportunity."

It is as if we were heading across the street but found ourselves caught right in the middle, equidistant from the curb we left and the one to which we want to go. When traffic is heavy, part of us wants to back up and part wants the excitement of dashing over. The critical shift comes when the desire to change is greater than fear of the process.

If we persist in our effort to steer a straight course, there is a breakthrough. We move away from indecision and take on the new project wholeheartedly. Something within us relaxes a little and we can bring forth our resources of intellect, imagination, and will. This is the point of the first awakening, when we learn to trust what is happening and perspective, objectivity, even a sense of humor emerge. This is the note *Fa*.

Encouraged and greatly enthused, we resolve to move forward, seeking a new path rather than simply accepting the one we received from others or from our own previous life experience. *Sol* represents the point of commitment, when we devote all our time, money, and energy to the new direction. It is the celebration, the gift along the way.

The next step, at *La*, sometimes seen as purification, tends to take us by surprise. We find that old doubts and fears resurface as it becomes necessary for us to give up anything from the old way of thinking that will not vibrate with the new. This state is often characterized by a sense of loneliness and loss, where it is easy to feel that we have temporarily lost our bearings or are caught in frustration. Jesus was speaking of this when he said,

"For those who want to save their life will lose it, and those who lose their life for my sake will find it" (Matt 16:25).

The key to the completion of the octave and the fruition of the project is our willingness to give up any personal desire to know exactly what should happen and our claim to and control of the results. The last step, therefore, is one of surrender, the point of second awakening, where synthesis and integration take place. This is the note *Si*. As we move onward to the *Do*, the goal, which was only dimly perceived at the beginning, then comes, with the help of knowledge and love from above, to its fullest possible realization.

Fernand Cabrol, in his article on the octave appearing in the *Catholic Encyclopedia*, recognizes the importance of the seven steps when he says:

> It is the number seven, not eight, that plays the principal role in Jewish heortology [study of religious festivals] and dominates the cycle of the year. Every seventh day is a sabbath; the seventh month is sacred; the seventh year is a sabbatical year...the feast of Pentecost was seven times seven days after the Pasch [Easter].
>
> However, the octave day, without having the symbolic importance of the seventh day, had also its role. The eighth day was the day of circumcision. The feast of the Tabernacles, which lasted seven days, was followed on the eighth by a solemnity which may be considered an octave.

Cabrol concludes by speaking at length of the adoption in Christian liturgy of the octave as an eight-day celebration beginning with a special feast day and continuing for seven more days.

As early as the fourth century, the festivals of Easter and Pentecost were given octaves and, from that time forward, the celebration of octaves is mentioned more frequently. This practice remains in the Christian liturgy of our own times, when not only the major events of the life of Christ but also those of many of the saints are especially remembered during the octave or the eight days following the consecrated day.

As we speak of the daily worship prescribed by St. Benedict, the plan of the liturgical year, and of the Mass itself, we do not mean to suggest that these forms of Christian worship were arranged by anyone sitting down to "make up octaves." It does seem, however, that the octave was part of the knowledge of the time and, as such, was definitely in the awareness of the early church fathers as they carried out their work over time.

Seven Hours by Day and One by Night

The octave, as may be seen in the Opus Dei described by St. Benedict in the Rule, is intimately connected with the movement of the sun during the long days of summer and the shorter days of winter. One may wonder why the octave of the Opus Dei begins at sunrise rather than with Vespers of the preceding day, a tradition established in Hebrew worship. Twentieth-century Christian martyr Dietrich Bonhoeffer, quoted by Robert Taft, speaks to this specifically:

> The Old Testament day begins at evening and ends with the going down of the sun. It is the time of expectation. The day of the New Testament Church begins with the break of day and ends with the dawning light of the next

morning. It is the time of fulfillment, the resurrection of
the Lord. At night, Christ was born, a light in darkness;
noonday turned to night when Christ suffered and died on
the cross. But in the dawn of Easter morning Christ rose in
victory from the grave...Christ is the "Sun of righteous-
ness," risen upon the expectant congregation (Malachi
4:2), and they that love him shall "be as the sun when he
goeth forth in his might" (Judges 5:31). The early morning
belongs to the Church of the risen Christ.[15]

Benedict's monks prayed the Office of Lauds at sunrise in thanksgiving for the dawn of a new day. The Lesser Hours of Prime,
Terce, Sext, and None provided moments when physical work or
study was stopped and everyone went to the oratory for prayer,
before which nothing else might come. During the daytime hours,
the movement of the octave may be seen in the instruction, challenges, and fulfillment provided by the work itself, whatever it
may have been. The human effort was to hold taut the line of
attention, watching and responding with care and love.

In the late afternoon, with the waning of the sun, the quality
of the hours changed. Vespers was a moment of serenity and peace,
resolution of conflict, and thanksgiving for the gifts of the day. This
was followed at night by Compline, a time for examination of conscience and asking for forgiveness for any sins committed.

One can view the challenge provided by the first octave
interval, *Mi* to *Fa*, as one that each individual monk needed to
overcome through obedience and attention to the task at hand.
However, the second interval, between *Si* and *Do*, was passed by
collective effort. The Office of Vigils, prayed by Benedict's
monks at the eighth hour of the night (approximately 2 A.M.),
was attended only by the monastic community and, of all the

hours, was the most musically elaborate. Benedict prescribes the chanting of fourteen psalms, an Ambrosian hymn, three lessons from scripture, and another reading plus responsories and petitions. This collective prayer, joined to the prayer of Christ himself, bridged the upper interval and prepared for the new octave to come at dawn.

The Liturgical Year

In the same way that St. Benedict and his followers observed the daily cycle of prayer, they also participated in a year-long cycle of liturgical events. This cycle came to be known as the Proper of the Time and provided for the commemoration of the principal events in the life of Christ. It also included all the Sundays of the year. Due to the fixed date of Christmas and the movable date of Easter, this cycle had to be adjusted annually. The Proper of the Time is distinguished from the Proper of the Saints, in which the feasts of individual saints, including the Virgin Mary, occur on specific and unchanging dates, many of which came into being centuries after the time of Benedict.

The Proper of the Time focuses on two major events in the life of Jesus Christ—his birth and his Resurrection—and are called the Christmas and the Easter cycles. For each there is a period of preparation, celebration, and prolongation. Christmas is prepared for by Advent and prolonged through Epiphany. Lent precedes Easter and the feasts of the Ascension of Our Lord and Pentecost follow it. The liturgical year as traditionally celebrated[16] begins with the first Sunday of Advent and concludes with the last Sunday of Pentecost,[17] after which a new cycle begins. As the various holy seasons are described and the yearly liturgical drama unfolds, it is important to realize that for the nuns and monks the events were not something that had happened several hundred years before. Rather, the religious entered into the celebration with their whole heart and soul, as if it were happening to them in present time. This is still the case today, when the same graces are received in the here and now.

In the life of Christ we see an event of cosmic importance. One therefore would not be surprised to find the octave again at work in the way that this divine life has been celebrated over the centuries in the traditional liturgy of the church. Bear in mind that the octave is a very flexible model, where the general sense of movement is more important than rigidly identifying a specific event with a specific note. Indeed, in the musical octave there is a diversity of possible tunings—Pythagorean, natural, tempered, and many others. Here, then, is one possible way to meditate upon the Proper of the Time.

Advent is the season of preparation which starts during the last week of November or the first week of December. Contrary to what one might conclude from observing the mad dash and frantic partying of the secular world at this time of year, Advent is intended to be a time of quiet reflection. Traditionally, the church saw the season as penitential; it was a moment when believers were invited to examination of conscience and inner preparation for the birth of Jesus. Today's church views Advent as a time of joyful and spiritual expectation. It has always been seen by Christians as a season of reflection on Christ's second coming. When Advent is associated with the bottom *Do* of the octave, it indicates preparation for the nativity of Jesus of Nazareth. The top *Do* will represent his second coming in glory at the end of time.

Christmas marks the first step or *Re* of the liturgical octave, the nativity from which all future events will flow. The birth of

Jesus represents the flowing together of two streams—one, pure love and compassion for the meek of the earth, the other bringing all the wisdom of the ages. The Gospel of Luke describes the innocent babe in the manger who draws to himself the simple shepherds and their flocks. The Gospel of Matthew indicates Jesus' royal lineage from Solomon and David, attracting the three magi or wise men who came from the East to worship him. The festival of the birth of Christ, originally celebrated in East and West on January 6, was changed in the fourth century by Western, Roman Christians to December 25th, a date near the winter solstice. It symbolizes not only the return of the sun after months of darkness but also the appearance of One who for millennia to come would light the whole earth with his radiance.

Christmastide, or the prolongation of the festival, lasts in the Roman West for twelve days until January 6, the Feast of the *Epiphany*. Epiphany means "manifestation," in this instance of the Holy Child to the magi who had traveled many miles to reach the stable where he was born. These were visitors who symbolized persons outside the Jewish faith and tradition who would also come to embrace the Christ. Epiphany also had additional significance as the day of Christ's baptism by John the Baptist in the Jordan River and the start of Christ's three years of ministry. The radiance of this holiday is represented by the note *Mi*.

After the Twelve Nights are over, everything feels lighter. It is as if the earth, having drawn all its vital energies into herself through the winter, finally awakens and opens once more. Spring is at hand. However, if we refer to the liturgical plan, we see that it is not possible to remain for long with the joy and peace of Epiphany; the octave moves on and more is required.

Ash Wednesday marks the beginning of Lent, when Christians traditionally take upon themselves penitence and special discipline. In the early church the imposition of ashes on the forehead was a way for persons guilty of serious public sins to show their repentance and also for catechumens—those learning the faith—to purify themselves and prepare for baptism at Easter. Eventually the whole community of the faithful began to receive the ashes as a reminder of their mortality and their need for forgiveness.

After Ash Wednesday, the *interval* of the octave, the forty-day period of *Lent*, begins. Represented by the note *Fa*, this is a period of intense effort. It offers individual Christians the opportunity to awaken and to reform their lives to be more in accordance with their own inner knowledge. At the same time, it is a season for deepening spirituality in union with the whole church. Lent has a very complex liturgy with a separate Mass for each day. Worshipers are asked to reflect on Christ's temptations and struggles, seeing in them a way to live their own lives with confidence and trust. The season concludes with the events of Holy Week: Palm Sunday, Jesus' triumphant entry into Jerusalem; the traditional Offices of *Tenebrae* (Latin: "darkness"), when a candle is extinguished after the singing of each psalm, symbolizing the impending sorrow of the crucifixion; Maundy Thursday (named for one of its antiphons, *Mandatum novum do vobis*, "I give you a new commandment," where the ritual enactment of Christ's washing of his disciples' feet takes place); Good Friday, the most solemn day of the Christian year, since it commemorates Christ's death on the cross, and yet one that looks forward with hope to the day of the Resurrection and is therefore called "Good"; Holy Saturday or Easter Eve, when the Paschal or Passover candle is lit to symbolize the light of Christ and when the catechumens receive holy baptism so as to be ready for the Easter celebration.

Occurring as the octave's brightest note, the *Sol*, Easter recalls Christ's Resurrection from the grave and is the most festive and joyous day of the liturgical year. The Mass begins with the words, *"Resurrexit, et adhuc tecum sum, alleluia,"* "I arose, and am still with Thee, alleluia." Christians celebrate not only Christ's defeat of death but also his unlocking of the gates of eternal life for all believers.

After Easter Sunday there are forty-nine days, i.e., another octave of Sundays, until the day of Pentecost. Along the way is the feast of the Ascension, corresponding to the octave note *La* which, itself, has an ascending quality. Here Christians celebrate the rising of Christ into the heavenly realms. He disappears from physical view but remains present to all creation.

Pentecost, at the note *Si* of the octave, is the longest period of the liturgical year, extending from the beginning of June until the start of Advent in December. The festival itself marks the moment when the disciples actually experienced the presence and power of Christ's Holy Spirit as tongues of fire descending upon them. Empowered to speak in many languages, they were instructed to spread Christ's message of love throughout the world. Individual believers were offered the possibility of experiencing for themselves the continuing gift of Christ's enduring presence. The length of the season (cf. the length of Vigils in the Divine Office, also at the note *Si*) indicates the importance of inner initiative and response through practice, something that Benedict emphasized over and over again in his faithful carrying out of the Opus Dei.

The feasts of All Saints' and All Souls' (November 1 and 2), when the church honors persons actually canonized and all faithful followers of Christ throughout the ages, were not part of the yearly liturgy at the time of Benedict. However, there is abundant evidence that pagan festivals long associated with the season were very much part of the awareness of the early Christians—the Roman *Feralia* to honor the dead and *Pomona*, the goddess of the harvest. It was seen as an *interval*, a time when the door to heaven was left ajar and people were more in touch with those who had died than at other moments of the year.

As the octave concludes and we look to a second Advent, we realize that there is no need for Christ to become incarnate again, to live among us in a physical body and pass through death. That was done once and need not be repeated. Christ is everywhere present. In spite of the darkness and negativity of the times in which we are living, his impulse is flooding the earth. It is for us to bring it to individual and collective consciousness and realization.

In his sixth-century Italian monastery, Benedict was already heir to an extraordinary liturgy. However, it was not simply the fact that he knew of it and shared in its formation but that he provided *the example of faithful practice* which is most important. In his words:

> We should always recall at such times the words of the Psalms: serve the Lord with awe and reverence,[18] and: sing the Lord's praise with skill and relish,[19] and: I shall sing your praise in the presence of the angels.[20] All of us then should reflect seriously on how to appear before the majesty of God in the presence of his angels. That will lead us to make sure that, when we sing in choir, there is complete harmony between the thoughts in our mind and the meaning of the words we sing.[21]

Across the centuries, that reflection on how to appear before the majesty of God in the presence of his angels has been the subject of a musical elaboration that even Benedict could not possibly have imagined. The gradual development of Western music from its beginning in the plainchant of Benedict's oratory to the majestic and varied choral and instrumental repertory with which we are beginning the third millennium will be traced in the chapters to follow.

4
Gregorian Chant and the Mass

"Sing the Lord's praise with skill and relish."
St. Benedict

Most Gregorian chant melodies were composed between 400 and 700 by anonymous composers working in praise of God. Words from the psalms carved on the portal of the church of Pont-Hubert near Troyes, France—

Non nobis domine, non nobis, sed nomini tuo da gloriam
Not to us, Lord, not to us, but to your name give glory[1]

—would certainly have expressed their view, since no specific person has ever been associated with the composition of a particular chant. One can only imagine the work that took place over the centuries to produce not just the music but also the textual unity of the Roman Catholic liturgy. Today, thirteen hundred years later, thanks in no small part to the restoration of the original melodies of most of the chants by the Benedictine Abbey of St. Pierre de Solesmes in France, we have a repertory that is one of the greatest of religious treasures.

Willi Apel, in his monumental book *Gregorian Chant*, tells us that as early as the year 150 Justin Martyr describes the Mass at Rome as consisting of "readings from the Old and New Testament, a sermon, an offering of bread and wine, prayer of the faithful, the kiss of peace, Eucharistic (thanksgiving) prayer, and communion."[2] He continues by saying that there is evidence in the writings of St. Augustine that Athanasius (299–373) "insisted that the Psalms should be sung with such moderate inflection that it sounded like speech rather than singing,"[3] so there is no doubt that chant was being practiced in the early centuries of the Christian era.

As was the case in the Liturgy of the Hours, most probably the first chanting at Mass was recitation on a single tone with one note to each syllable of text:

EXAMPLE 1: FESTAL TONE CHANTED ON A SINGLE NOTE

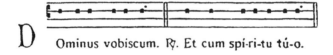

D Ominus vobiscum. ℟. Et cum spí-ri-tu tú-o.

The Lord be with you. And with your spirit.

From the *Liber Usualis*, Benedictines of Solesmes, eds. (Tournai, Belgium: Desclée & Co., 1952), 98. Permission granted by les Editions de Solesmes, Abbaye Saint-Pierre de Solesmes, Sablé-sur-Sarthe, France.

As time went on, the priest or cantor added some embellishment, either additional notes at the beginning of the line or before the main recitation tone or a change of pitch up or down at the end.

EXAMPLE 2: ANOTHER ANCIENT TONE

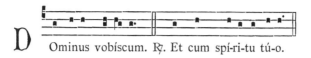

Ominus vobíscum. ℞. Et cum spí-ri-tu tú-o.

The Lord be with you. And with your spirit.

From the *Liber Usualis*, Benedictines of Solesmes, eds. (Tournai, Belgium: Desclée & Co., 1952), 108. Permission granted by les Editions de Solesmes, Abbaye Saint-Pierre de Solesmes, Sablé-sur-Sarthe, France.

Eventually it became usual to sing two to five notes to some syllables, creating more interest and variety in the musical expression of the text:

EXAMPLE 3: *VENI SANCTE SPIRITUS,* SEQUENCE FOR PENTECOST

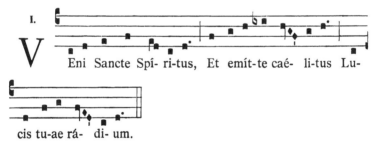

Eni Sancte Spí- ri-tus, Et emít-te caé- li-tus Lu-

cis tu-ae rá- di- um.

Come Holy Spirit, and send forth a ray of your heavenly light.

From the *Liber Cantualis*, Benedictines of Solesmes, eds. (Sablé-sur-Sarthe, France: Abbaye Saint-Pierre de Solesmes, 1978), 63. Permission granted by les Editions de Solesmes, Abbaye Saint-Pierre de Solesmes, Sablé-sur-Sarthe, France.

Since the purpose of the singing was to cause the holy words of scripture to penetrate the worshiper's entire being, the lines were often repeated and sung in different ways: alternation of cantor or priest and congregation; division of the congregation to sing alternate verses and then come together for the refrain. This chanting back and forth was called "antiphonal" (as distinguished from "antiphon" which, as already explained in connection with the Office, was a short text sung before a psalm or canticle) and was introduced in Milan by St. Ambrose (340–397).

After the beginning of the fourth century and particularly the Edict of Milan in 313, which raised the Christian faith to the status of an officially recognized religion, stopping the persecution of its members, the liturgy began to flower. Already highly developed in the churches of Palestine and Syria, it was first organized in Rome by Pope Damasus I (366–384) after the model of the church of Jerusalem and as advised by St. Jerome. Less than half a century later Pope Leo I (440–461) instituted a cycle of chants for the whole liturgical year.

According to a number of historical indications, the task fell to Pope Gregory I to regulate the order of the Masses and, to a large extent, the arrangement of the chants within them that is still observed today. Although the repertory was not actually written by Gregory but rather by anonymous composers over several centuries, he doubtless took an active part, either personally or through directives given to his subordinates, in the final reorganization of the chants. In this he was continuing and concluding a work to which a number of earlier popes had already contributed. The traditional naming of the entire chant repertory as "Gregorian Chant" in honor of his far-reaching contribution is therefore very well deserved. Willi Apel summarizes:

It would mean that a considerable repertory of melodies had accrued during the centuries before Gregory for whom it remained to collect the melodies, to assign them a definite position in the cycle of the year, and possibly to add some new ones for feasts that he introduced; all this, of course, with the *proviso* that these things were done under his direction rather than by himself in person.[4]

Certainly the work of St. Gregory set the stage for a much more elaborate rendering of chant. This began during his lifetime and continued throughout the seventh century, reaching its height in the twelfth century with the rather ornate and, to our ears, perhaps florid chant of Léonin and Pérotin at the cathedral school of Notre Dame de Paris. This style of singing, named "melismatic," called for the singing not of just one or a few but of many notes to a single syllable. An example of this was the *Alleluia*, in which the syllable "a" was often extended by a long melisma.

EXAMPLE 4: ALLELUIA

Alleluia

From the *Liber Cantualis*, Benedictines of Solesmes, eds. (Sablé-sur-Sarthe, France: Abbaye Saint-Pierre de Solesmes, 1978), 19. Permission granted by les Editions de Solesmes, Abbaye Saint-Pierre de Solesmes, Sablé-sur-Sarthe, France.

In the year 600 Gregory is said to have ordered the singing of the *Alleluia* chant by his *schola cantorum* at every Sunday Mass during the whole year, except for the period of Lent, a practice still observed today.

The Modes of Gregorian Chant

One of the ways that Gregorian chant achieves subtlety and variety is through the use of more modes or arrangements of the successive tones of an octave than is common in the music of the Classical and Romantic periods, to which our ears are more attuned. We are used to hearing a scale referred to as "major"—

Do   **Re**   **Mi Fa**   **Sol**   **La**   **Si Do**

—with its pattern of two whole steps followed by a half-step, three whole steps followed by a half; or "minor," the simplest version of which is

La   **Si Do**   **Re**   **Mi Fa**   **Sol**   **La**

or whole step, half step, two whole steps, half step, two whole steps.

The eight principal modal scales of Gregorian chant were formally classified by musical theorists only in the tenth century, when most of the repertory was already in place. These scales were divided into sections of pentachord (five consecutive notes) and tetrachord (four consecutive notes), where the last note of the first segment was also the beginning note of the second:

Re	Mi	Fa	Sol	La	Si	Do	Re
	PENTACHORD			SHARED NOTE		TETRACHORD	

The scales could be sung beginning on any convenient pitch, but it was essential to respect the half-tones between *Mi* and *Fa* and between *Si* and *Do*, retaining whole steps in all other places.

The modal scales were arranged in pairs. The odd-numbered scales were referred to as "authentic" and began with the notes *Re*, *Mi*, *Fa*, or *Sol*. In these, a pentachord was followed by a tetrachord:

1)	*Re*	*Mi*	*Fa*	*Sol*	*La*	*Si*	*Do*	*Re*
3)	*Mi*	*Fa*	*Sol*	*La*	*Si*	*Do*	*Re*	*Mi*
5)	*Fa*	*Sol*	*La*	*Si*	*Do*	*Re*	*Mi*	*Fa*
7)	*Sol*	*La*	*Si*	*Do*	*Re*	*Mi*	*Fa*	*Sol*

SHARED NOTE

Chants written in modes 1, 3, 5, or 7 can often be identified by the fact that their *final* note is *Re* in the case of mode 1, *Mi* in mode 3, *Fa* in mode 5, and *Sol* in mode 7. One can also expect that the music will tend to be written in the eight-note range immediately above this important note.

The four even-numbered or "plagal" modes involve a transposition where the tetrachord comes first, followed by the pentachord. Mode 2 would therefore begin with the shared note of mode 1 and the note *Re* (final in the actual chant melody) would be placed not at the beginning but near the middle of the octave:

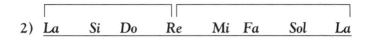

2) *La*   *Si*   *Do*   *Re*   *Mi*   *Fa*   *Sol*   *La*

Likewise, for modes 4, 6, and 8, related to modes 3, 5, and 7 in the same way:

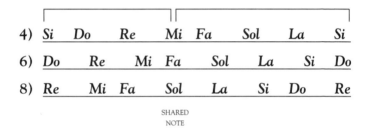

4) *Si*   *Do*   *Re*   *Mi*   *Fa*   *Sol*   *La*   *Si*

6) *Do*   *Re*   *Mi*   *Fa*   *Sol*   *La*   *Si*   *Do*

8) *Re*   *Mi*   *Fa*   *Sol*   *La*   *Si*   *Do*   *Re*

SHARED
NOTE

A rule of thumb for identifying which of the eight modes applied to a specific chant would be, first, to look at its final note and, second, to notice whether the rest of the notes of the chant are above this note, i.e., represented as higher on the musical staff. If they are, the chant is in the authentic modal scale. If some of the notes are below this final note, and the final note is roughly in the middle of the vocal range, one can assume that the modal scale is the corresponding plagal version.

It is important to remember that the Gregorian repertory was chanted for five centuries by singers who learned it all by heart without the aid of a written text. The growth was organic, using and combining basic formulae elaborated through the years. Since the classification of chants was done after the fact, not every one fit perfectly into the modal system.

The majority of the chants have a range of seven, eight, or nine notes, with narrower ranges found among the older and simpler chants. Melodic progressions generally move by step up or down the notes of the modal scale. Skips of a third in either direction up or down (*Do* to *Mi* or *Do* to *La*) are common. The smoothness and uniformity of the melodic line thus created makes larger skips all the more noticeable when they do occur. Intervals of more than five notes are very rare.

Due, no doubt, to the fact that melodies from any one particular mode often accompany scriptural texts that are extremely different in meaning, there is hesitation among scholars to speak of the "mood" created by the modes. There is more general agreement that certain modes find their way into certain parts of the Mass liturgy such as the *Gradual*, which is often rendered in modes 2 and 5.

However, the Benedictine monks of Solesmes note that each of the eight modes was considered the expression of a particular emotional or moral climate, perceptible to those who sing them on a daily basis and, taken collectively, are a musical embodiment of the spiritual values inherent in the entire liturgy of the church. They are listed by Solesmes in this way:[5]

Mode 8   *Perfectus* (perfect)

Mode 7   *Angelicus* (angelic)

Mode 6   *Devotus* (devotional)

Mode 5   *Laetus* (joyous)

Mode 4   *Harmonicus* (harmonious)

Mode 3   *Mysticus* (mystical)

Mode 2   *Tristis* (interior)

Mode 1   *Gravis* (noble or dignified)

It is fascinating to note the similarities between the qualities cited for these modes and the notes of the octave already mentioned in chapter 3, pages 63–67: *Do* provides the foundation from which further development comes; *Re* is the start of the activity, where challenge is presented and inner resources are required; *Mi* is a subtle, lighter note, full of possibilities; the harmonious, yet somewhat poignant note *Fa*, reached after the first interval is crossed, prepares the way for the strongest, most joyful note *Sol*, which follows; *La*, the note of surrender, ascends to the *Si* which, like the angels, leads the octave or the event across the final interval to its completion in the perfect *Do* above.

Can all of this actually be heard in the ancient chant melodies? What is the effect that they have on spirit, mind, and body? If, like Benedictines, we faithfully practice them, praying as we sing, we will no doubt come to an answer. Most likely the knowledge will come with the final note, at the very end.

The Rhythm of Chant

Whatever indication we may have of the rhythm of the early Gregorian chant comes to us from chant books written by scribes in the tenth century and later, notably in the churches of Laon, Chartres, and St. Gall. These books were used primarily by conductors as an *aide mémoire* before and during performance. Singers, on the other hand, did not need a written reference, since the chants had been committed to memory.

Texts from the liturgy were written in these books and above the words were placed certain musical signs, called "neumes."

EXAMPLE 5: NEUMES

╱   the *virga*, "green twig or rod," stands for one long note, higher than the preceding;

⌐ or ╱ the *podatus*, "foot," meant two short or two long notes ascending;

⌐ or ⌐ the *clivis*, "slope," indicated two short or two long notes descending.

Slightly more complicated configurations were:

√ the *porrectus*, "reached out," which represented two short notes and a long, in a high-low-high pattern; and

∧ the *torculus*, "wine press," the same, but low-high-low.

The pattern of the neumes showed the conductor the configuration of hand movements to use while directing. There are no specific indications either of pitch or of the size of the musical interval, since the chant was sung in any convenient range and the melody was well known to all the singers. A number of well-documented historical sources indicate that the chant of the seventh and eighth centuries may well have used a system of long and short values, corresponding with the accentual patterns of the Latin language. The effect of this early, more measured, proportional rendition is that of walking very close to a line from which the music departs—sometimes in highly decorated melismas —but to which it regularly returns. This chant, with its robustness and solidity, might remind us of the Romanesque churches—

solid, rectangular, and dark—built to contain and retain the spiritual Presence within their walls. The churches sit squarely on the earth and are firmly grounded in it. Both architecture and chant proclaim the same spirituality: "Thy will be done on earth," which is perhaps why the Emperor Charlemagne was said to have been so enamored of the style. This type of chant reached its height in the tenth century, but began soon to decline.

For more than eight hundred years, Gregorian chant has been sung in equalist rhythm, where each note is of approximately the same length and indivisible, and where textual accentuation is noted more by nuances of stress than by length. The equalist chant, so beautifully exemplified in the singing of the monks of the Abbey of Solesmes, has a more ethereal, celestial quality that is reflected in the tall, light-filled, soaring Gothic edifices of the French cathedrals of Chartres and Bourges.

By the end of the twelfth century, the chant repertory was so extensive that it could no longer be committed to memory. The result was a need to create a staff, eventually of four lines, where neumes, now written considerably larger, could be placed to indicate pitch. This innovation, due largely to the work of Benedictine monk Guido d'Arezzo, will be further discussed in chapter 5. As time went on, the chant books no longer provided any precise indication of rhythm.

The Mass

We may safely assume that the early liturgists had at their disposal the words and prayers of Holy Scripture; chant forms from simple, intoned, to highly melismatic; and various hymns and other melodies, some of which antedated the Christian era and came from the Jewish tradition. All of these elements, and the awareness of the symbolism of number, would have contributed to the beauty and majesty of their work. We now will turn to the way everything came together in the structure of the Mass.

In order to understand the Mass, we must first have a clear idea of the participants, their function in the unfolding of the liturgy, and the type of chant normally assigned to them. The person presiding over the gathering, the priest or celebrant, was the spiritual leader. He was not necessarily expected to have particular musical competence and therefore the chants he sang were not difficult and often simply intoned. Likewise, the congregation's responses were limited to short, easily memorized acclamations. Playing an intermediate role were the various ministers—the acolytes who assisted the priest at the altar, the readers, and the deacon, who did have the musical role of proclaiming the gospel reading. Music that required more expertise was offered by soloists or by the *schola cantorum*, all of whom were obliged, in the absence of any written form of the music, to learn everything by heart through listening to it.

The sung parts of the Mass have traditionally been divided according to whether they were the textually unvarying part of every celebration, the "Ordinary," or whether they changed from one week and from one feast to another, the "Proper." Today when we think of the music of the Mass, especially its elaborate renditions by composers such as Schubert, Bach, or Beethoven, we are generally referring only to the Ordinary—the *Kyrie, Gloria, Credo, Sanctus,* and *Agnus Dei*. From the point of view of Gregorian chant, however, Mass meant Proper—the *Introit, Gradual, Alleluia, Offertory,* and *Communion*—which indicated the special meaning of each celebration and accompanied the Eucharist. The change in point of view occurred about 1300 when the items of the Ordinary were preferred for polyphonic composition, because a particular *Kyrie* or *Gloria* could be sung on almost every feast, while a particular *Introit* or *Gradual* could be used only once a year.

Based on psalms and scriptural antiphons, the parts of the Proper were in general use in Western Europe probably as early as 500 and, by the time of Gregory, these chants were fully standardized. Quite a different situation is presented by the Ordinary: These chants are non-psalmodic and originated in the Eastern Church. The *Kyrie*, *Gloria*, and *Sanctus* are very ancient, but the *Agnus Dei* came into the West only at the end of the seventh century. The *Credo*, although textually dated from the fourth century (it was approved by the Council of Nicaea in 325; hence the name "Nicene Creed") was not made part of the musical liturgy of the Roman Mass until after the year 1000. Except for the *Gloria*, the Ordinary chants were all originally sung by the congregation, a practice reflected in the simple style of the oldest melodies. Later, in the ninth century, they were taken over by the *schola* and consequently more elaborate renditions appeared.

The Liturgical and Musical Celebration

Historically the essence of the Mass was to re-present for the worshipers Christ's sacrificial death on the cross and to invite them to share in this sacrifice by participating in the prayers, offering thanks, and receiving the consecrated elements. In this way participants were taken up into the paschal mystery and, by being united to the risen Christ, received the forgiveness of their sins and eternal life. The laity received the Eucharist only under the species of bread. The liturgical renewal of the Second Vatican Council in the early 1960s, however, emphasized not only the sacrificial aspect but also the celebration, as in the early church, of the whole community of worshipers. It allowed reception of communion under both species of bread and wine on feast days and Sundays, at least as an option. Whereas the spirit of the Mass before Vatican II was individualistic, the council restored emphasis on the creation by the Eucharist of unity within the whole Christian community.

For nearly all of its existence the Mass was enacted in Latin, a language unfamiliar to most worshipers (as another innovation of the council, the use of vernacular language was introduced); therefore the Mass was more easily appreciated through the emotions and senses than through the intellect. Worshipers were ushered into a world where the sound of chant, the taste of the elements, the sight of the altar and ceremonial robes, and the smell of incense all contributed to the experience of holiness. By listening and giving full attention to the Mass, they were brought through successive steps away from the worldly and into more direct contact with the mysterious, divine presence of Christ.

We may suppose that the Mass, like all medieval religious works of art, was not constructed according to the personal wishes or desires for innovation of liturgists but, rather, according to number and proportion in much the same way as the buildings wherein it was enacted. Here the musical model of the octave may be helpful in understanding the progression of the steps of the Mass and the effect upon the worshipers that these steps most probably were intended to have.

In his book *Gregorian Chant and Its Place in the Catholic Liturgy*, Jos. Smits van Waesberghe offers a tabulation of the Mass as traditionally celebrated before the time of the Second Vatican Council, which we have adapted for present purposes.[6] It includes two basic parts, the Preparation and the Sacrifice:

THE MASS

A. THE PREPARATION

EXHORTATION TO TRUST WITH CONFESSION OF GUILT

1. Entrance of the priest *(Introit)*	Song of the *schola cantorum*
2. Prayer for Mercy *(Kyrie)*	Song of the people and/or *schola*
3. Praise and Thanksgiving *(Gloria)*	Song of the people and/or *schola*
4. Request for favors *(Collect)*	Song of the celebrant
5. Reading *(Epistle)*	Song of the assisting clergy
6. Intermediate chants: *Gradual* + *Alleluia* or *Tract*, sometimes *Sequence*	Songs of the *schola*
7. Gospel reading (Sermon)	Song of the assisting clergy
8. Confession of Faith *(Credo)*	Song of the people and/or *schola*

B. THE SACRIFICE

OFFERING OF THE BREAD AND WINE

OFFERTORY

9. *Offertory* chant	Song of the *schola cantorum*
10. Song of Homage *(Preface* with *Sanctus)*	Song of the celebrant, people/*schola*

CHANGE OF THE BREAD AND WINE INTO THE BODY AND BLOOD OF CHRIST

CONSECRATION

11. Song of Welcome *(Benedictus)*	Song of the people/*schola*
12. Lord's Prayer *(Pater Noster)*	Song of the celebrant
13. Prayer for Mercy *(Agnus Dei)*	Song of the people/*schola*

RECEIVING OF THE SACRED OFFERING

COMMUNION

14. Thanksgiving *(Communion)*	Song of the *schola*
15. Closing prayers	Song of the celebrant
16. Dismissal *(Ite, Missa est! Deo gratias)*	Song of the assisting clergy/ people/ choir

Nos. 2, 3, 8, 10, 11, 12, 13, and 16 in bold type are "fixed prayers," the Ordinary of the Mass; nos 1, 4, 5, 6, 7, 9, 14, and 15 are "variable prayers," the Proper of the Mass.

It is useful to notice that the whole Mass includes two smaller eight-step octaves, each complete within itself. When dealing with medieval constructions, whether physical as in buildings or abstract as in musical liturgy, one should not so much strive for consistency as for meaning to be found in analogies and metaphors. In some instances, the eighth step of one octave, for example, might represent the simple first step of the next; at other times it might not.

Steps 1–8 were traditionally referred to as the Mass of the Catechumens, those learning the faith. They included the Way of Purification (steps 1–2), wherein the aspirant humbled himself through prayers of supplication, and the Way of Illumination (steps 3–8) where the effort was one of listening to the teachings of Christ and forming oneself in accordance with them. Once the work of the first octave had been completed, not only in the Mass but in the life of the man or woman over time, then he or she was ready to pronounce the Confession of Faith and move on to the next octave, called the Way of Union, through participation in the sacrifice. Those who were insufficiently instructed and had not yet been baptized might have left before step 8. Steps 9–16, occurring after the interval and bridged by the worshipers' own declaration of faith in God and in Christ, were called the Mass of the Faithful or the Holy Eucharist.

The *Do* represents the persons who have arrived in their various states of preparation and are ready to begin to experience the transformations that will be brought about by the liturgy. They form a community of faith whose purpose is to listen to God's word in scripture and celebrate the Holy Eucharist.

The Introductory Rites, where the whole octave progression begins to work, may be considered the note *Re*. The *Introit* summons the worshipers to the feast. It is the welcome at the beginning of Holy Mass. Sung by the *schola* during the time that the priest and assistants move either from the sacristy or the back of the church to the altar, it provides the *leitmotif* of the sacred drama. The thoughts of the assembled congregation are directed by the *Introit* to the mystery of the particular feast and to its place in the liturgical year. Musically, it includes an opening antiphon and a psalm verse followed by the traditional *Gloria Patri* ("Glory to the Father"). As the names of the members of the Holy Trinity are mentioned, all bow in reverence.

After the *Introit* comes a litany, the *Kyrie eleison* ("Lord have mercy") chanted three times by the *schola* and people, followed by the *Gloria in excelsis Deo* ("Glory to God in the highest"), or song of the angels at the birth of Christ, when the *schola* and congregation again sing together. The *Collect* or prayer particular to the day, sung by the priest, completes the Introductory Rites. The theme of the liturgical celebration has been stated and the worshipers have been led into the realization that they are in God's presence.

The note *Mi* is the step where the path of the liturgical octave is further clarified. Instruction is provided by readings from the epistles—letters from Jesus' apostles to the early Christian churches —and from one of the four Gospels. Between these readings are musical responses, which tended over time to become longer and more elaborate.

These intermediate chants are normally two in number and chosen for seasonal appropriateness: in Lent there are a *Gradual* and a *Tract*, during the period after Easter, two *Alleluias*, and during the rest of the year, a *Gradual* and an *Alleluia*.

The texts selected for the *Gradual*, rather than being one connected piece of scripture, often consist of a combination of a number of short verses taken from widely different parts of the

Bible. This way of selecting texts assures that the words chosen will both fit the day's celebration and be well-suited for a musical setting.

The *Alleluia*, a joyous melismatic song of praise traditionally sung by the skilled musicians of the *schola*, goes back to the fourth century, for St. Augustine (353–430) describes how the "alleluia singer," when he had no more words with which to praise God, sings notes without words to express his jubilation.

> If somebody is full of joyful exultation,... he bursts out in an exulting song without words; *or* For whom is this jubilation more proper than for the nameless God? ... And since you cannot name him and yet may not remain silent, what else can you do but break out in jubilation so that your heart may rejoice without words, and that the immensity of your joy may not know the bounds of syllables.[7]

The tremendously heightened expressiveness of the *Graduals* and *Alleluias* makes them particularly moving to those unaccustomed to listening to chant. Those more familiar with chant find in them some of the anonymous composers' most daring and original work.

The *Tract*, which replaces the *Alleluia* during Lent and on other somber occasions, is confined to a few psalm verses sung straight through without antiphons or response. The standard *Tract* melodies, believed characteristic of a very early type of plainsong, are relatively few, but they have been adopted to cover a large number of scriptural texts. It is unusual in the liturgy for one chant to follow another immediately as is the case with the chants between the lessons. Ancient lectionaries provide evidence that there were not two but three lessons that these chants served to separate—a lesson from the Old Testament, then the Epistle, then the Gospel. The singing of the Gospel by the deacon (assistant clergy), followed by the priest's commentary upon it, the Sermon or Homily, closed the Liturgy of the Word.

The *Credo* ("I believe"), which would come at the octave interval, was then spoken by all those who professed the faith and who would continue on to the second part of the Mass. Those who had not yet been baptized would sometimes leave at this point in the Mass. The formal use of the *Credo* is documented for the first time in Constantinople in the early sixth century and not long thereafter in Spain. It appeared in the Roman-Frankish Mass first in 794 but was not formally adopted in its musical form in Rome until 1014. Although the text itself was fairly long, it was most often rendered very simply through the repetition of four standard formulae which recur, in different combinations, with each "verse" of the text.

In the same way that Lent prepares the way for Easter, the *Offertory* chant and Eucharistic Prayer (*Preface* with *Sanctus*), the note *Fa* of the octave, lead to the consecration, the most sacred moment of the Mass, represented by the brilliant note *Sol*. Sung by the *schola* while the elements of bread and wine were brought in procession and laid upon the altar, the *Offertory* consists of psalm verses receiving a rich melismatic presentation like the *Gradual*. These chants are distinctive for their often extremely ornate melodies and also for the frequent repetition of both text and melodic phrases that goes on while the offerings are being presented.

When the gifts have been received, the priest begins the Eucharistic Prayer as preparation for the Communion. The *Pref-*

ace acknowledges that praise and thanks are owed to God and leads directly into the *Sanctus* ("Holy, holy, holy") and *Benedictus* ("Blessed"), both originally congregational songs and later chant for the choir. The text of the *Sanctus* and *Benedictus* combines passages from both the Old and New Testaments: From the vision of Isaiah, who saw the angels calling to each other, is taken "Holy, holy, holy is the Lord of hosts: the whole earth is full of his glory"; and from the Gospel of Matthew, the words, "Blessed is he that cometh in the name of the Lord: Hosanna in the highest." These texts inspired a tremendous diversity of forms and styles, making them perhaps the most interesting chants of the Ordinary.

Once the Eucharistic Prayer is complete, the celebrant sings the *Pater Noster* ("Our Father"), the prayer that Jesus himself taught his disciples to say. Asking that God's will be done on the earth as it is in heaven, this prayer is represented by the *La* of the octave. It is the point where worshipers surrender "the kingdom, the power, and the glory" to God.

The *Agnus Dei* ("Lamb of God"), a prayer for mercy not introduced in Rome until around 700, accompanies the breaking of the bread. Placed at the note *Si* of the Mass octave, it prepares the worshipers for the Communion, whose grace comes from God alone. In the early church the bread was in the form of loaves that had to be broken into many pieces before being distributed among the communicants. This ceremony is known as the "fraction." If the communicants were numerous, the fraction took a long time and, of course, so did the chant. Later, when unleavened bread baked in small wafers was substituted for loaves, and when it was no longer the custom for the congregation to receive communion, the role of the *Agnus Dei* became less important.

The *Communion* consists of a brief antiphon appropriate to the day, followed by a psalm and sung antiphonally by the *schola* while the bread is actually being distributed. Although it is simple in style, similar to the *Introit*, it falls within the interval between the *Agnus Dei* at *Si* and the conclusion of the octave at *Do*. As such it was the other crucial interval, filled in this instance only by divine grace. Here, given the careful preparation by the liturgical celebration and their own willingness, the worshipers may experience divine union with Christ.

At the conclusion of the Mass, the upper *Do* of the octave, there are closing prayers and the deacon sings the words *Ite missa est* ("Go, you are dismissed"), from which comes the word "Mass," indicating that the worshipers are to return to serve in the world, renewed in faith by what they have experienced.

5
Skilled Benedictine Musicians

"Work with good spirit."
St. Benedict

The repertory of Gregorian chant represented by the Opus Dei and the Mass showed astonishing development between the seventh and twelfth centuries. In this the Benedictine monks and nuns played a role of enormous importance. Their principal contributions were the offering to God of unceasing prayer and praise and their example of faith in the preeminence of the unseen world of Spirit. Their concern was establishing a path of communication, personal as well as collective, with what was essentially invisible. For this, their instrument was the daily chanting of the choral liturgy.

As Georges Duby states in *The Age of the Cathedrals*, his outstanding interpretation of the art and society of Western Europe during the years 980–1420:

> Words led to God. Melody led to him still more directly
> because it afforded glimpses of the harmonic chords of
> the divine creation and because it gave the human heart

a way to mold itself to the perfection of the divine intentions. In chapter 19 of his *Rule*, Saint Benedict quoted Psalm 138, "before the gods will I sing praises unto thee." In his view, the choir of monks prefigured the heavenly choir, did away with the partitions separating heaven and earth, and was in itself an introduction into the ineffable and the realm of uncreated light.[1]

When St. Benedict composed the Rule in the sixth century, he intended it as a guide for the monks of his abbey at Montecassino. He had no plan to form an order, much less one that would spread the sacred liturgy across the whole of Western Europe. However, his words and, more, perhaps, the example of his continual remembrance of God in prayer, proved powerful enough to withstand the test of time. While whole civilizations were in movement and turmoil, the monks, through fidelity to their vow of stability, stayed still and in place, at least to the extent that the ravages of invasion and plague would allow.

The strong intention of prayer and praise enunciated by Benedict slowly found adherents across Western Europe during the seventh and eighth centuries but it was not until Benedict's Rule and monastic way of life were formally associated with the secular reform movement pursued during the long reign of the Emperor Charlemagne (768–814) that almost universal acceptance of them would be claimed. Charlemagne wanted to establish a single empire uniting all the Roman and Germanic peoples, based on his own authority and that of the religious leaders in Rome. He envisaged a return to the culture of the Roman Empire, but this time, thoroughly Christianized. The plan was to enlist the participation of as many monasteries of Western Europe as possible in following the Rule of St. Benedict, recognized by the emperor as being the most effective instrument of discipline and unification available.

A decisive step in the propagation of the Rule and its observance came with the work of St. Benedict of Aniane (born 750) who, though originally from Burgundy, founded his own monastery at Aniane, near Montpellier in the south of France. This monastery grew into a large feudal institution of some three hundred monks. From Aniane, Benedict sent groups to other houses in the area, thereby forming a congregation. His interest in organizing monasteries attracted the attention of Louis the Pious, Charlemagne's son. Louis built a royal monastery called Inde near the palace at Aachen in Western Germany where Benedict presided over a community whose observance became a model for the whole empire. Benedict was authorized to enforce a standard observance in the monasteries of France and Germany. Monks were sent to Inde for training and inspectors could then visit their monasteries to secure compliance.

Unfortunately, the efforts at unification were short-lived. Benedict of Aniane died in 821. During the remainder of the ninth century, the empire was torn apart by strife among Louis's sons and the continent was ravaged by waves of Norse and Saracen invaders. Charlemagne's great project was never achieved. However, when it again became possible for monasteries destroyed by war and political dissent to rebuild, it was upon a foundation laid by Benedict of Aniane.

The Abbey of Cluny

The decline following the reforms of Benedict of Aniane was countered with the foundation of new centers of Benedictine monasticism in the tenth century. The first and most prominent of these centers was Cluny. The story of the acquisition of land for this prominent abbey has been researched by Therese Schroeder-Sheker:

> In the early fall of 909, a wise Burgundian monk named Berno was summoned to visit the aging William III, Duke of Aquitaine, a seasoned aristocrat. The death of William's only son had left him in pain and without an heir. In preparing for his own death, William reasoned that he could not take his vast worldly possessions with him, and decided to found a monastery free from all secular and immediate diocesan jurisdiction. The duke urged Berno to choose freely from his lands. When the monk cited the sheltered valley of Cluny, with ancient forests and quarries of red and grey stone, William choked. This was the finest hunting ground in the entire duchy! Quietly, the Benedictine inquired, "Which would serve you better before God, the prayers of the monks or the baying of hounds?" William, stinging with desire and attachment, hesitatingly conceded and composed the charter for a new French monastery that was to change the face of Europe.[2]

The Abbey of Cluny was conceived as independent from intrusions of either kings or bishops and was linked only with the church of Rome. Free from any pressure outside the Order, its monks maintained the privilege of designating their own abbot.

Soon Cluny began to draw other houses under its influence. These houses, instead of forming separate families, remained in absolute dependence upon the central abbey. Thus there arose a kind of feudal hierarchy that eventually extended across Burgundy, Provence, Aquitaine, and into Spain along the pilgrim route to Santiago de Compostela. By the eleventh century it reached northward to the rest of France and the British Isles and eastward to Italy and Poland.

During the first two hundred and fifty years of its existence, Cluny was governed by a series of remarkable abbots: Saints Odo (927–942), Mayeul (948–994), Odilo (994–1049), Hugh (1049–1109), and Peter the Venerable (1122–1157). These monastic leaders, whose sanctity was equal to their discretion and administrative ability, brought Cluny to its zenith of influence and prosperity in the mid-twelfth century when it was second only to Rome as the center of the Christian world.

The abbey church of Cluny measured 555 feet in length, consisted of five naves, a narthex, or ante-church, and several towers. It was regarded as one of the wonders of the Middle Ages, a splendid setting for the enactment of the liturgy. Raoul Glaber, an eleventh-century monk and chronicler, let us know that Masses were celebrated from the earliest hours of the day until the time for bed. So elaborate and demanding was the schedule of liturgical celebration that the monks of Cluny did little else. The manual labor so characteristic of Benedictine practice in previous centuries was assigned to laypeople, who were not involved so much in liturgical and private prayer as they were in service to the monastery. These Masses and hours were a particular vision of the endless hymn of praise owed to the Lord of all. The chant repertory naturally grew by leaps and bounds. The idea of combining the services commemorating all those who had died into a single liturgical rite, All Souls' Day, is credited to Cluny's monks.

From the beginning of the tenth century through the middle of the twelfth, Cluny was like an extremely bright lamp shedding light on music, scholarship, the arts, and, of course, worship. It was, without a doubt, the most important institution in Europe at the time. However, seeds of reform were again being sown. The desire for a return to the simpler, more solitary way of St. Benedict brought about changes in the monastic world and produced a number of new "orders" and observances alongside established houses such as Cluny. The most successful of these was that of Cîteaux, founded in Burgundy in 1098 and made famous by St. Bernard. His followers, the Cistercians, emphasized greater solitude and poverty and a more literal observance of the Rule of St. Benedict than that at Cluny.

Of continuing importance as well were Benedictine foundations in Italy, Germany, France, and Spain, and the extremely vigorous Benedictine revival in Normandy and England in the eleventh and twelfth centuries.

Guido d'Arezzo

The expansion of the Gregorian chant repertory that took place from the seventh to the ninth centuries was given the means both for its own preservation and also for its full flowering in the polyphonic music to come largely through the work of the Camaldolese Benedictine monk Guido d'Arezzo.

One of the most important music theorists of the Middle Ages, Guido was born in France around the year 998. He became a member of the Order of St. Benedict in the monastery of St. Maur des Fossés, near Paris, where he received his education. Early in his career he observed the confusion that prevailed in the teaching of the Gregorian repertory. As the number of chants grew, the system, which indicated only the relative direction of the melody—whether a particular word or syllable should be sung higher or lower than the preceding—was becoming hopelessly inadequate. The neumes were vague and could not indicate the precise pitch required. Singers often took as long as ten years to become proficient, learning everything by rote through practice.

Guido's first attempts at musical innovation made him unpopular with his brethren in the Order and led to his moving first to the monastery of Pomposa near Ferrara, Italy, and then, in about 1030, to one in Arezzo. It was during the next decade that Guido, working with spirit and against objections, perfected a new system of notation that brought dramatically increased order and clarity into the singing and teaching of chant.

Gradually Guido's innovative work received recognition both in the monasteries and from the reigning Pope John XIX, who, in about 1033, invited Guido to come to Rome to exhibit his antiphonary (book of antiphons) containing the liturgical melodies transcribed with his own staff notation from the chant books previously used.

Guido helped musicians of his own time and generations to come through the use of two very important innovations. First, he taught a system for singing called "solmization," whereby each note of the scale was associated with the initial note of each phrase of a Latin hymn to St. John the Baptist:

> **Ut** *queant laxis*
> **Re**sonare fibris*
> **Mi**ra gestorum*
> **Fa**muli tuorum,*
> **Sol**ve polluti*
> **La**bii reatum,*
>
> *Sancte Joannes.*

EXAMPLE 1: HYMN TO ST. JOHN THE BAPTIST

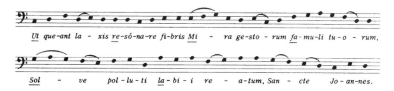

Ut que-ant la - xis re-só-na-re fi-bris Mi - ra ge-sto - rum fa - mu-li tu - o - rum,

Sol - ve pol - lu - ti la - bi - i re - a-tum, San - cte Jo - an-nes.

That thy servants may, with relaxed voice, proclaim the wonders of thy deeds, absolve the sins of their unclean lips, O holy John.

From Richard H. Hoppin, *Medieval Music* (New York: W.W. Norton & Company, 1978), 63.

Once the hymn was well learned, the singers could recall its lines and would have a clear idea of how each note was supposed to sound in relation to the other notes, respecting the position of the semi-tone between *Mi* and *Fa*. At first, Guido's hymn accounted for only the first six notes, beginning with "Ut," but soon hexachords, or six-note sequences, were begun on other notes—on *Fa* and on *Sol*—expanding the original scale to eight notes and creating other scales. Eventually the word "Do" from **Dominus**, "Lord," was substituted for "Ut" and, with the full-fledged development of the seven-note scale, "Si" was added, taken from the S of **Sancte** and the old-style J (written as I) of **Johannes**.

Guido's second achievement was the introduction of a practical system of musical notation solving what had previously been an almost impossible problem of indicating pitches on parchment.

In the treatises of Greek musicians, letters of the alphabet were used to designate the notes of the octave: C *(Do)*, D *(Re)*, E *(Mi)*, F *(Fa)*, G *(Sol)*, A *(La)*, B *(Si)*, and C *(Do)*. Before Guido, scribes sometimes wrote these letters close to or relatively far above the words of the text to indicate lower or higher notes respectively. Sometimes they would draw a line upon which they placed one of the letters and from which they then measured the distance of the melodic steps above or below.

Guido no doubt found two such lines already in use, a red one where F or *Fa* was placed and a yellow one for C or *Do*, indicating the placement of the tones represented by these letters. His great improvements were the addition of two more lines to the existing ones and the utilization of the spaces between the lines for succeeding notes as well.

This system of staff notation has been used ever since. The reason why only four lines were used instead of the five we now employ is that these four lines and five spaces (three between, one below, and one above) were considered sufficient for the range of the average Gregorian melody.

The clef written at the beginning of the staff indicated the placement of the notes. There were two clefs in use, the *Do* clef, two dots, one above and one below the line, indicating the position of *Do*, and the *Fa* clef, a note with descending tail, followed by two dots, marking the place of *Fa*.

EXAMPLE 2: DO AND FA CLEFS

Both of the clefs were movable. The *Do* clef was placed sometimes on the second line, often on the third line, and very often on the top line. The *Fa* clef was generally on the third,

EXAMPLE 3: NEUMES OF SQUARE NOTATION AND THE MODERN EQUIVALENT

From the *Liber Usualis* (Tournai, Belgium, 1952: Desclée & Co.), xx and xxj.

sometimes on the top. The shifting of the clef was merely to enable melodies of different ranges to be written on the staff without adding more lines, a conserving of precious parchment.

With regard to the neumes themselves, certain conventions applied. Notes in ligatures were read from left to right, and two notes aligned vertically were read from bottom to top. Example 3 provides illustrations of neumes, indicating the way chant is presented today by the Benedictine monks of Solesmes, along with the modern equivalent.

Now try your skill at reading part of the great hymn for Pentecost *"Veni Creator Spiritus"* as it appears in the *Liber Usualis*. If you learn to sing it as the monks do, you will begin with the syllables *Sol, La, Sol, Fa, Sol, La, Sol, Do, Re, Do:*

Example 4: Veni Creator Spiritus

Come, creator Spirit, and visit the minds of your faithful. Fill with heavenly grace the hearts you have created.

From the *Liber Usualis*, Benedictines of Solesmes, eds. (Tournai, Belgium, 1952: Desclée & Co.), 885. Permission granted by les Editions de Solesmes, Abbaye Saint-Pierre de Solesmes, Sablé-sur-Sarthe, France.

Guido's system of solmization and his reworking of the musical staff gave an impetus to musical progress that lasted throughout the Middle Ages. His influence can be appreciated as well in the development of polyphonic music by his advocacy of contrary motion of the voices—the upper ascending while the other descends—as opposed to the parallelism normally employed with both parts moving in the same direction.

Hildegard of Bingen

Before leaving the Middle Ages, it is important to consider the rich contribution of one other Benedictine, Hildegard of Bingen, whose music has been rediscovered only in the last twenty years.

Benedictine Abbess Hildegard of Bingen was certainly one of the most creative people to emerge from the twelfth century. Known in her own day across Europe from England to Byzantium, she was the personal adviser of bishops, popes, and kings. She traveled extensively and carried on an impressive correspondence with both secular and ecclesiastical authorities. Research during the past fifty years reveals that this extraordinary woman compiled treatises on natural history, involved herself deeply with religious and social issues, was abbess of three different convents, and composed poetry, drama, and music of transcendent beauty and originality. In all of these she never presented herself as a scholar operating through her own knowledge but always as the instrument of God's will.

The rediscovery of Hildegard was due in no small part to the critical scholarship of the nuns at St. Hildegard's Abbey in Eibingen, Germany. In 1928 Sister Maura Böckeler published a German translation of Hildegard's most famous work, the *Scivias* (from *Sci vias Domini*, "Know the Ways of the Lord") and in 1956 two other Eibingen nuns, Marianna Schrader and Adelgundis Fürkötter, produced an important historical and paleographic study that established beyond doubt the authenticity of Hildegard's works.

The first composer whose biography is known, Hildegard was born in Bermersheim near Alzey in Rheinhessen (the German Rhineland between the towns of Trier and Mainz) in 1098. From a very young age she was aware of a brilliance that filled her visual field at all times while not affecting or impairing her natural vision. She interpreted this as "the radiance of the living Light of God." This *visio* or gift of extraordinary inner sight later provided visions of great symbolic complexity, interpreted for her by a voice from heaven. Hildegard maintained that it was this voice, speaking in Latin, which dictated her books and letters.

At the age of eight, Hildegard was sent by her parents to be educated at a convent community within the walls of the Benedictine monastery of Disibodenberg, at the confluence of the Glan and Nahe rivers in Western Germany. There she was placed in the care of the recluse Jutta von Spanheim, who taught her to sing from the Latin Psalter and to play the ten-stringed lyre.

After Jutta's death in 1136, Hildegard herself became the abbess of the convent community and, five years later, when she was nearly forty-three years of age, she was told by God in a vision that she should begin to write and speak of her spiritual insights. The result was the *Scivias*, which contained twenty-six of her visions and commentaries on them. Bernard of Clairvaux, to whom she wrote for confirmation of the value of her work, was immediately supportive as was Pope Eugenius III who, in 1147, sent Hildegard a letter of apostolic blessing and protection.

To accommodate the increasing number of nuns joining the community, Hildegard began the building of an independent convent for women at Rupertsberg in Bingen, where the Nahe

River flows into the Rhine. Against the opposition of the monks of Disibodenberg, who would have preferred to retain her talents, she and twenty other nuns transferred to Rupertsberg in 1150. During the years Hildegard spent at this location she wrote her second book of visions, *Liber divinorum operum*, "Book of Divine Works." In spite of the fact that she was often physically ill, she made three long journeys to various religious communities in the Rhineland, where she preached at monasteries and cathedrals.

In 1165 Hildegard made one final acquisition of property, this time the convent of Eibingen, near Rüdesheim, which became a daughter house across the river from Rupertsberg. Hildegard was the leader of this institution as well and crossed the Rhine twice a week to attend to its affairs.

As an aside it can be mentioned that it was on this third site that a new Benedictine Abbey of St. Hildegard was founded in the nineteenth century by Prince Karl of Löwenstein, who resolved to see the tradition of Hildegard's convents revived at a historic site. Today sixty Benedictine sisters live in the reconstituted abbey under the supervision of the abbess, who is the thirty-eighth successor to Hildegard herself. The nuns sing the Opus Dei in Latin, carry out research into Hildegard's life, and care for visiting pilgrims.

Hildegard's existence was fraught with conflict and tension culminating in an incident that occurred in 1178, just a year before her death. At the time, Hildegard and her nuns were denied the right to sing the liturgy. The alleged reason for this was their refusal to exhume a man buried in the cemetery at Rupertsberg. This man had been excommunicated but later reconciled to the church and given the last rites. The canons disputed the man's reconciliation and the problem continued.

Finally, Hildegard wrote an impassioned letter to the prelates of Mainz presenting music and the singing of the liturgy as humanity's bridge to the heavenly harmonies. She pointed out that the Devil tries to prevent the adoration of God by silencing music sung in his praise. Strongly inferred was the association of the prelates with evil itself! Here is what she wrote to them:

But when the devil, man's great deceiver, learned that man had begun to sing through God's inspiration and, therefore, was being transformed to bring back the sweet-ness of the songs of heaven, mankind's homeland, he was so terrified at seeing his clever machinations go to ruin that he was greatly tormented. Therefore, he devotes himself continually to thinking up and working out all kinds of wicked contrivances. Thus he never ceases from confounding confession and the sweet beauty of both divine praise and spiritual hymns, eradicating them through wicked suggestions, impure thoughts, or various distractions from the heart of man and even from the mouth of the Church itself, wherever he can, through dissension, scandal, or unjust oppression.

Therefore, you and all prelates must exercise the greatest vigilance to clear the air by full and thorough discussion of the justification for such actions before your verdict closes the mouth of any church singing praises to God or suspends it from handling or receiving the divine sacraments. And you must be especially certain that you are drawn to this action out of zeal for God's justice, rather than out of indignation, unjust emotions, or a desire for revenge, and you must always be on your guard not to be circumvented in your decisions by Satan, who drove man from celestial harmony and the delights of paradise.[3]

The interdiction was lifted in March of 1179 and Hildegard died on September 17 of the same year at the age of eighty-one.

Hildegard's Music

Hildegard's accomplishment in music was at the heart of her creativity, expressing the full authority, intelligence, and striking originality of her genius. She often apologized for her lack of formal training, but it was probably this fact that allowed her the freedom of expression and experimentation so evident in her work. For Hildegard, music was something totally natural, quintessentially human, the natural expression of the inner life and love of God. As Nancy Fiero puts it:

> Hildegard's music can only be fully understood in the light of all her work. The beauty and depth of theme found in her theology, philosophy, cosmology, and medicine, can all be found condensed in her music as in a jewel. For Hildegard as for the medieval, music was an all-embracing concept. It was the symphony of angels praising God, the balanced proportions of the revolving celestial spheres, the exquisite weaving of body and soul, the hidden design of nature's creations. It was the manifest process of life moving, expanding, growing towards the joy of its own deepest realizations and a profound unity of voices singing the praises of God here on earth. It was beauty, sound, fragrance, and the flower of human

artistry. Over three hundred times in her writings Hildegard uses music to illuminate spiritual truths.[4]

Although Hildegard's original and unorthodox style moved medieval chant far beyond its prescribed norms, it is still clear that her compositions were intended for integration with the convent liturgy. Hildegard composed many songs for saints that were revered locally such as Rupert and Disibod. She was also inspired by themes more universally recognized, such as the martyrdom of St. Ursula, the majesty of the divine kingdom, and the purity of the Virgin Mary. The texts of her poems and music make clear her strong sense of the interdependence of all created things and her interpretation of the entire universe in spiritual terms.

The monasteries provided an ideal milieu for Hildegard's endeavors, offering a scriptorium where her music could be copied, a skilled *schola* capable of singing it, and the daily liturgy as occasions for its performance.

Hildegard's songs, although imbued with the clarity and beauty of the liturgy she knew so well, represent, in many ways, a radical departure from traditional rules. Her pieces sometimes illustrate a range as large as two and a half octaves, putting quite a strain on the voice of the average singer. It is as if she traverses the scales up and down with as much ease as she moved between the world of spirit and the world of mundane affairs. Musical phrases are stretched and contracted to create an impression of soaring arches. A particular hallmark of Hildegard's own style, her musical "signature," is a melodic leap of a fifth (*Do* to the *Sol* above) followed by a jump of a fourth upward (from the *Sol* to the *Do* above), which has been compared to humanity's ascension from earth to heaven.

The sequences and hymns in Hildegard's repertory are generally neumatic, with only two or three notes per syllable, but her antiphons and responsories are melismatic in the extreme. Nothing in her compositions is totally musically predictable. She tends to use three different modes, on D, E, and C, and draws on a relatively small number of motifs that she repeats, with ingenious variations, in every piece in that mode.

Regarding Hildegard's specific compositions, Barbara Newman concludes:

> Hildegard did not initially plan to compose a song cycle any more than she planned to write a trilogy. Her music had its origins in the concrete liturgical life of Rupertsberg, and only when she had composed a substantial body of lyrics—probably in the late 1150s—did she decide to collect all her songs and arrange them in a systematic order. After making this decision, she continued to compose new pieces that were incorporated in the cycle only after her death.[5]

These poetical-musical works are entitled *Symphonia armonie celestium revelationum*, "Symphony of the Harmony of Celestial Revelations." In this instance, "Symphony" meant not only the joyful harmony created by a chorus of voices singing together but the spiritual unity monastics seek when singing together—integrating mind, heart, and body, healing discord, and celebrating heavenly harmony here on the earth. The *Symphonia* included seventy-seven songs together with the musical drama *Ordo Virtutum*, or "Play of Virtues."

The *Ordo Virtutum*, an enactment of the eternal battle between good and evil, was probably composed for the dedication in 1152 of Hildegard's independent convent in Rupertsberg. The score required sixteen women to sing the roles of the virtues and one man, probably the only male in the community, Hildegard's secretary Volmar, to play the spoken part of the Devil. Hildegard saw the Devil as essentially the enemy of harmony, the one trying always to steal it away from humanity. He was therefore the ultimate unmusical spirit and was given a shrill speaking voice, experienced as a raucous interruption in the otherwise blessed world created by the music.

The play brings these allegorical figures to life. We can hear them operating on behalf of the human soul, *Anima*, fighting off the temptations of the Devil. In the beginning, Anima is seen as clothed in white robes ascending to paradise. However, before she has been received there, the Devil gains her attention and she is sidetracked into promises of renown in the world.

The virtues complain loudly over the Devil's apparent victory. He insults them vociferously but cannot harm them. Each one—humility, charity, fear of God, obedience, faith, hope, innocence, and so on—introduces herself. Anima returns from her experiences in the world, downtrodden, wounded, and embittered, and calls on the virtues for help. They raise her up and give her once more her robes of immortality. The Devil makes one more appeal but is finally confounded.

It is not known if Hildegard used instruments to accompany the *Ordo* or her songs. However, it is certain that she affirmed their use and saw them as an effective means to soften the heart and direct it toward God. Modern recordings of Hildegard's music use them very effectively to heighten and further dramatize her message.

Hildegard's inspiration was clearly based on her daily chanting of the liturgy with her Benedictine communities. She saw

The marvels of God
are not brought forth
from one's self.

Rather,
it is more like a chord,
a sound that is played.

The tone does not come
out of the chord itself,
but rather,
through the touch
of the musician.

I am, of course,
the lyre and harp
of God's kindness.

God says:
 Ever
 you are
 before my eyes.

God, I am your opus.
Before the beginning of time,
already then,
I was in your mind.

God has created me.
God is my Lord,
 having dominion over me.

God is also my strength,
 for I can wish to do nothing
 good without God.

Through God I have living spirit.
Through God I have life and movement.
Through God I learn, I find my path.

If I call in truth, this God and
Lord directs my steps;
setting my feet to the rhythm of
his precepts.[6]

—Hildegard of Bingen

that many times a day people lose their way or find themselves off-center. Music was the best way to retune the mind and heart to God. It is significant that Hildegard should be one of the most appealing models in our own contemporary search for wholeness and spirituality.

From Hildegard to Solesmes

The thirteenth to the nineteenth century is sometimes character-ized as a difficult period in Benedictine monasticism. In the grad-ual change from feudalism to urban life, the economic base of the monasteries was ruined; both ecclesiastical and secular princes impoverished the monasteries by demanding revenues and by interfering in their internal affairs; the Black Death and the Hun-dred Years' War severely decreased the numbers in many houses. The number of people choosing the monastic vocation declined, so much so that the houses could not be maintained at their for-mer level of vigor and fervor. Some monasteries, bent upon pre-serving tradition, were unable to meet the challenge of the new learning, the new economy, and the aspirations of a developing society. Monks continued to chant the Divine Office, but they moved away from the original discipline of Benedict into a more sentimental and less faithful observance. The result was that some candidates came to the monastery more to find an easy life than to seek God. However, it is important to note that not all houses were overcome by the various negative influences around them. At all times there existed abbeys where fervent and disci-plined work was carried on.

The fifteenth century saw the rise of a new institution, the joining together of various abbeys, which strengthened monastic life in some areas. Abbot Luigi Bargo (d. 1443) became abbot of St. Justina in Padua in 1408 and reinstituted a more regular discipline. Recruits were so numerous that he was able to reform many existing abbeys, which were united in a congregation in 1419. All the monasteries of Italy and Sicily eventually joined this congregation, which later called itself the Cassinese Congregation.

Also very well organized was the Congregation of Bursfeld, approved in 1446. Its influence spread so rapidly in north Germany that in the sixteenth century it included some two hundred houses. In Spain the congregation of Valladolid embraced the monasteries of Castile and some in Catalonia, and eventually spread to Mexico and Peru.

In the early seventeenth century there was a remarkable revival of monasteries in France with the founding of the congregations of St. Vannes and especially St. Maur. The congregation of St. Maur came to include nearly two hundred monasteries and produced two of France's greatest scholars, Mabillon (1632–1707) and Montfaucon (1655–1741). At the same time, a notable Cistercian reform was undertaken at the Abbey of La Trappe by the famous Armand-Jean de Rancé, founder of what became the Trappist observance.

In the eighteenth century monasteries again experienced difficult times. In France the Revolution destroyed all the monasteries and that tendency spread across Europe. A century later, however, monasteries overcame past obstacles and began, with spirit, to rebuild themselves. A number of Benedictine and Cistercian monastic leaders took steps to ensure that the Rule of Benedict would continue to strongly influence monastic life. A pioneer of this Benedictine revival was Prosper Guéranger who, in 1833, reestablished monastic life and liturgical practice at

Solesmes, France. The reforms of Dom Guéranger and others had far-reaching effects, especially in music.

The Abbey of Solesmes

In the nineteenth century the chant repertory occasioned much controversy due to the flowery decorations added by composers and choral leaders through the years. A movement began to renew this ancient music by returning it to an earlier, purer state. Many monks and scholars contributed to this effort of restoration, but its main proponents were the monks of the Benedictine Abbey of St. Pierre de Solesmes, situated between Le Mans and Angers in northern France. When the abbey itself was restored in 1833 after many vicissitudes, its abbot, Dom Prosper Guéranger, set for himself and the abbey the task of reinvigorating liturgical practice and particularly Gregorian chant.

The scholar monks adopted a modern, scientific method in their research, traveling widely and copying all the manuscripts available in the libraries of Europe. Dom Guéranger and his monks wished to restore the lost accent and rhythm of Gregorian chant and in restoring the text of the chants laid down the principle to which they have always adhered: that when various manuscripts of different periods agreed on a version, that was the most correct.

Early efforts at restoration carried out by Dom Jausion (1843–1870) and Dom Pothier (1835–1923) emphasized the necessity of referring to the ancient manuscripts for melodic line and notation, and the need for good phrasing in performance. In 1900 Dom André Mocquereau (1849–1930) became leader of

the work. His far-reaching contribution was the personal training of the Solesmes Schola which, through the years, influenced
many others. With his publication of *Paléographie musicale*, containing photographic reproductions of scores of manuscripts from
all the principal libraries of Europe, a far greater degree of accuracy was possible than with mere transcripts that might contain
copyists' errors. These reproductions have been brought together
and are studied at Solesmes even to our day. The *Graduale
Romanum*, the *Antiphonale*, and the *Liber Usualis* prepared there
are used throughout the world, wherever chant is sung.

This work at Solesmes received the highest possible recognition in 1904 when Pope Pius X entrusted the monks there with
preparing an official Vatican edition of the church's chant, appoint-
ing a commission for the purpose with Dom Pothier as president.
Today the community of Solesmes has achieved a world-wide
reputation for its erudition, its devotion to monastic and liturgical studies, and the magnificent rendering of chant by its *schola
cantorum*.

Benedictine Hymn Writing since Vatican II

The Second Vatican Council of the early 1960s brought about
dramatic changes in both the liturgy and the music of the
Catholic Church. The Mass, previously said in Latin, could now
be celebrated in the vernacular language. Music from other
Christian traditions could be included in worship services and
renewed emphasis was placed on the participation in singing not
only of the clergy and choir but of the entire congregation.

The challenge of these new directives began to be specifically
addressed in 1966 through the formation in Latrobe, Pennsylva-

nia, of the Benedictine Musicians of the Americas (BMA)—an organization headed by then-Abbot Rembert Weakland, O.S.B. and including a group of like-minded Benedictine musicians. Like their predecessors Guido d'Arezzo, the abbots of Cluny, St. Hildegard, and the monks of Solesmes, these composers and writers exercised great creativity, this time in order to incorporate new high-quality texts into the post-Vatican II liturgy.[7]

Since the founding of the BMA, forty to one hundred Benedictine and Cistercian musicians have been meeting biennially and have in some years been joined by Camaldolese and English monks as well. Their meeting provides a forum for the sharing of liturgical compositions by fellow Benedictines, discussion of issues and concerns relevant to Benedictine ministers of music, and experience of the joy of gathering to praise God in song. In 1979 BMA members prepared and published a hymnal in commemoration of the sesquimillennium (1500th anniversary of St. Benedict's passing), A *Benedictine Book of Song*.[8] This first Benedictine hymnal was followed in 1992 by a second.[9]

Illustrative of the flowering of Benedictine music at the end of the twentieth century was the work of Cecile Gertken, (1902–2001), a sister of the Order of St. Benedict, St. Joseph, Minnesota, who devoted her talents to preserving the ancient chant melodies, fitting them to English translations of the new Mass texts, and to translating and adapting antiphons and hymns for the Divine Office.[10]

As we move into the new millennium, the work of Sr. Delores Dufner, O.S.B., the foremost female Roman Catholic hymn text writer in the United States at this time, serves as a shining example of the pairing of familiar melodies with new texts that are in conformity with the insights of Vatican II.[11] Sr. Delores, also working at Saint Benedict's Monastery, St. Joseph, Minnesota, has selected melodies beloved by worshipers and durable over time and has used them as the foundation for her inspired and creative textual expression of renewed liturgical themes such as: the church as the entire, diverse people of God called to lifelong conversion and mission; the centrality of the word of God; the Eucharist as thanksgiving and nourishment for living the gospel; the role of the Holy Spirit in the ongoing renewal of the church; the Liturgy of the Hours as the prayer of the whole church; and baptism as the foundational sacrament. Her hymnbook, *Sing a New Church*,[12] which offers forty-eight inclusive language texts set to hymn tunes in the public domain, provides a valuable resource for musicians, liturgy planners, homilists, composers, and all who wish to sing with joy the praise present in their hearts. Here are two examples of Sr. Delores Dufner's work based on Gregorian chant, taken from *Sing a New Church*, pp. 65 and 115.

EXAMPLE 5: JESUS, GOD AMONG US

JESUS, GOD AMONG US

Delores Dufner, OSB   ADORO TE DEVOTE, 11 12 11 12

1. Je - sus, God a - mong _ us, pres-ent in the bread, By your bro-ken
2. With this bread is plant - ed seed of what will be: Joy and feast-ing

1. bod - y shared, hun-gry hearts are fed. Bread of our _ thanks-giv - ing,
2. with our God ev - er - last - ing - ly. Har-vest o - ver - flow - ing,

1. bread of life di - vine! May we be your bod - y shared, of your love a sign.
2. ban - quet of de - light! Hap-py at this ta - ble spread, all whom you in-vite.

EXAMPLE 6: WHEN THE UNIVERSE WAS FASHIONED

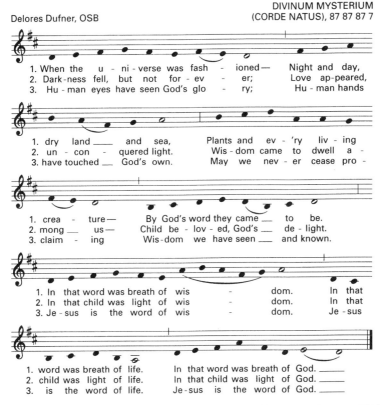

WHEN THE UNIVERSE WAS FASHIONED

DIVINUM MYSTERIUM
(CORDE NATUS), 87 87 87 7

Delores Dufner, OSB

Another original and uplifting contribution to music of the church also inspired by the directives of the Second Vatican Council comes from Weston Priory, founded by Benedictine

Abbot Leo Rudloff in Weston, Vermont, in 1953. Abbot Leo, since his years as a young monk studying at Sant'Anselmo in Rome, was active in the currents of monastic renewal, particularly a retrieval of the original spirit of Benedictine monasticism that strove to eliminate the distinction between choir monk and lay brother and favored a simpler, more accessible celebration of monastic liturgy.

The musical result has been a number of vibrant songs composed originally by the monks for the enrichment of their own liturgical celebration but, in recent years, recorded and widely distributed by the priory as tapes and CDs. The production of each song is genuinely collaborative, with one brother composing the lyrics and another the melody and arrangement. Coming from field, garden, and forest, from craft shop, kitchen, and office, each brother lends voice and spirit to the singing. The words of the songs are sometimes taken from scripture, sometimes poetic expressions of day-to-day situations; all are seen as the expression of the common life in Christ of the brothers and of the many laypeople who often worship with them. The instrumental accompaniments to the music are extremely varied and lively.[13]

Benedictine Monasticism and Creativity

Having read of the astonishing work of Benedictine musicians through the centuries, one may have reason to wonder about the wellsprings of their creativity, especially when they were working so often against tremendous difficulty and opposition. We may readily ask what there was about the monastery that so favored not only musical, but also many other types of innovation.[14]

Benedictine scholar Jean Leclercq, O.S.B., has explained the elements of monastic life most conducive to creativity as *"otium"* or "leisure" and the possibility of working in collaboration with others.[15] *Otium* does not mean leisure in the sense of idleness. Rather, it connotes attitudes and activities best designated by the word *hesychasm*, taken from the Eastern Church tradition, which is understood as repose of spirit. Leclercq describes this quality as

> well-informed, balanced, religious, holy, spiritual, studious; it is interior, total, perpetual; it is diligent, sustained, productive, vigorous, and delectable. It is characterized by stability, to which it is sometimes thought to be assimilated, for it is the opposite of constant change and indeed the remedy for human changefulness. It is serenity. It does not preclude the interior movements of the human spirit but directs them toward a transcendent goal: to God, in whose eternity they may share even now.[16]

The particular kind of beauty seen in monastic art is active and dynamic and yet always contains an element of interior silence and peace of heart. The work itself is seen as a continuation of the creative activity of God, bestowing on whatever the form may be—music, architecture, painting, sculpture, handwork—a supplemental beauty. The quality of the particular endeavor is often the result of the labor of a small group working anonymously with charity, humility, organization, and obedience presupposed. Leclercq characterizes the result as a "pure, simple, peaceful style of art. It is neither tragic nor exuberant, like the art bred in other schools of spirituality. Rather it is calm and brings a sense of peace because it is conceived by those who, at the price of laborious leisure, strove to be at peace with themselves."[17]

Conservation and Transmission of Culture

Benedictines, because of their love of the word gained through *lectio divina*, have made distinguished contributions as authors, theologians, historians, and chroniclers. Jean Leclercq characterizes their writings as often poetic, having sometimes greater value because of their power of suggestion than because of their clarity or precision.[18] Monastic exegesis is literal and mystical, interpreting scripture by scripture itself, the letter by the letter. The Bible is seen not primarily as a source of knowledge, of scientific information, but rather as a means for salvation. Patristic and monastic commentary is addressed to the whole being, aiming to touch the heart rather than to instruct the mind.

Benedictines have always loved and valued books. From the days of St. Benedict, it has always been assumed that every monastery would have a library. These libraries often served as a cultural Noah's Ark, preserving classical pagan as well as Christian literature. Without the diligent work of monastic librarians, much of our knowledge of classical antiquity would have been lost. The musical manuscripts, so patiently copied and bound by thousands of unknown monks and nuns, would never have been available for study at Solesmes.

In the monastic scriptorium, a whole group of monastics engaged in book making: the head of the workshop, the copyists, correctors, rubricators (the red letter men), painters, illuminators, and binders. Each book was a group effort, often requiring deciphering from a poorly preserved manuscript. Each text required very careful revision, correction, collation, and criticism. Monks and nuns became very proficient in preparing parchment that would last a long time and in creating metal and leather bindings.

With the arrival of the printing press, many monasteries stopped copying, but others moved on and set up their own printing presses. A present-day example of the conservation of manuscripts, a work requiring tremendous patience and accuracy, is provided by the microfilming project of Saint John's Abbey in Collegeville, Minnesota.

Shortly after World War II—a war that had been catastrophic for many precious documents—Pope Pius XII asked Father Colman Barry of Saint John's Abbey to address the further fate of manuscripts. When Father Colman assumed presidency of Saint John's University, he presented to the Louis W. and Maud Hill Family Foundation a plan that called for the preservation on microfilm of the classical and medieval handwritten cultural heritage of Western civilization—every text and book written before the invention of printing.

With funding provided by the Hill family, the Hill Monastic Manuscript Library (HMML, pronounced "Himmel," which is the German word for heaven) was founded in 1965.[19] Since then, it has sent teams of researchers and technicians to film more than twenty-five million pages from nearly ninety thousand volumes in libraries throughout Europe, the Middle East, and North Africa. Today HMML is one of the largest and most comprehensive archives of medieval and Renaissance sources in the world.

Benedictine monks and nuns have also chosen a tremendous variety of other ways and means for supporting themselves and, in so doing, have imparted to their products a quality known worldwide. More traditional fruits of their labors have been wines, beer, and specialty foods, fine handwork, and clothing. A new initiative being undertaken by creative monks at Christ in the Desert Monastery, in Abiquiu, New Mexico, is the design of web pages. Because the location of the monastery is so remote and there are no telephone lines nearby, they use cell phones for their Internet access!

Wherever they are, Benedictines provide a sense of community, continuity, ingenuity, and careful endeavor. It is important to remember, however, that the primary focus is not on the result, however excellent that may be, but on using the work as a means for seeking God.

6
Our Lady and Her Music

"Respond to God's love by obeying God's will."
St. Benedict

Virgin venerated throughout the world,
Mother dear to the human race,
Woman, marvel of the angels,
Mary, most holy.
By your blessed virginity you have made all integrity sacred,
and by your glorious child-bearing
you have brought salvation to all fruitfulness.
—St. Anselm[1]

Devotion to the Blessed Virgin Mary plays an extraordinary role in Benedictine monasticism. Like the Opus Dei and the Mass, this love for Mary has inspired countless flowerings in the liturgy and in devotional music throughout the centuries. We need, therefore, to spend time with "Our Lady," in order to understand the depth and power of her continuing influence.

Whereas the New Testament is replete with references to the life and teachings of Christ, explicit references to Mary are not numerous. Nonetheless, her being, placed somewhat behind the scenes, quietly and effectively pervades monastic life. The same radiance and beauty seen in Christ, called by Abbot Patrick Barry "the light that makes us like God or shapes us into the likeness of God"[2] can also be seen in Mary.

Monastics view Mary, the Mother of Christ and also his perfect disciple, as the model for the contemplative life. The virtues so much extolled by St. Benedict—the capacity to listen, obedience to God's will, and humility in carrying it out—are clearly exemplified in Mary's life as revealed in scripture.

Monastics see Mary as the ideal of consecrated virginity. The monk or nun wishes union with Christ alone and desires the celibate life in order to achieve an even deeper intimacy with God through Christ. He or she also reveres Mary as the Holy Mother, a being of unfathomable love, sensitivity, and self-giving, the supreme example of what it means to be human. She is the servant of the Lord, totally obedient to his word. Monastics perceive in her example the truest, most authentic creativity and fruitfulness, a way of life governed by following God's will in service to the human family.

Mary in Church Tradition

Virgin and mother; model of goodness and refuge of sinners; the humble handmaiden of the Lord and the powerful advocate of the poor, the oppressed, and the marginalized; the woman of lowly estate and the Queen of Heaven—Mary is a being of infinite flexibility and malleability, encompassing roles that may, at first, seem contradictory. Across the millennia Mary has been able to assume the vocations that would most closely answer the needs both of the developing and changing church and its individual believers.

Pope John Paul II speaks to the apparent lack of specifics about Mary's life by suggesting that it is in fact "a special intention of the Holy Spirit, who desired to awaken in the church an effort of research which, preserving the centrality of the mystery of Christ, might not be caught up in details about Mary's life but aim above all at discovering her role in the work of salvation, her personal holiness, and her maternal mission in Christian life."[3]

A close following of the liturgy reveals that the same three nativity events are celebrated for Mary as for her divine Son: on December 8, the Immaculate Conception of Mary, who is believed, like Jesus, to have been always free of original sin; Mary's own birth on September 8; and Mary's presentation at the temple on November 21. The feasts, however, which connect her most intimately with the life of her Son, receive most attention liturgically and in subsequent musical treatment.

The Annunciation, celebrated on March 25, recalls the angel Gabriel's announcing to Mary that she will carry in her womb God made man and associate herself forever with his redemptive work. It extols Mary's putting aside her fears at the enormity of the task, her receptivity to what she perceives as the will of God, and the humility of her response, "Behold the handmaid of the Lord: be it done unto me according to thy word."[4]

Three months after the Annunciation, Mary goes to the village of Ain Kerem in Judah to visit her cousin Elizabeth, miraculously pregnant in her old age with John the Baptist. When Elizabeth hears Mary's words of greeting, her baby leaps in her womb. Recognizing the holiness of Mary and the sacredness of her vocation as Mother of the Lord, Elizabeth speaks the words, "Blessed art thou among women, and blessed is the fruit of thy womb."[5] This meeting of Mary and Elizabeth is known as the Visitation and is now marked in the liturgy by a celebration on July 2, although for centuries it was celebrated on another date. Luke 1:46–55 records the words ascribed by the evangelist to Mary, her *Magnificat*, one of the most beautiful and powerful of scriptural texts:

Magnificat anima mea Dominum,	My soul proclaims the greatness of the Lord,
et exultavit spiritus meus	and my spirit rejoices
in Deo salutari meo.	in God my Savior.
Quia respexit humilitatem	For he has looked with favor
ancillae suae:	on his lowly servant:
ecce enim ex hoc beatam	from this day all generations
me dicent omnes generationes:	will call me blessed:
Quia fecit mihi magna, qui potens est,	the Almighty has done great things for me,
et sanctum nomen ejus.	and holy is his Name.
Et misericordia ejus a progenie	He has mercy on those who fear him
in progenies timentibus eum.	in every generation.
Fecit potentiam in brachial suo:	He has shown the strength of his arm:
dispersit superbos	he has scattered the proud
mente cordis sui.	in their conceit.
Deposuit potentes	He has cast down the mighty
de sede,	from their thrones,
et exaltavit humiles.	and has lifted up the lowly.
Esurientes implevit bonis,	He has filled the hungry with good things,
et divites dimisit inanes.	and the rich he has sent away empty.
Suscepit Israel puerum suum,	He has come to the help of his servant Israel,
recordatus	for he has remembered
misericordiae suae:	his promise of mercy:
Sicut locutus est ad patres nostros,	The promise he made to our fathers,
Abraham et semini ejus in saecula.	to Abraham and his children for ever.

Musical Rendering of the Magnificat

The *Magnificat* is sung at Vespers (evening prayer) each day in Benedictine monastic communities. It is also the liturgical text most often given polyphonic rendition from the mid-fifteenth to the beginning of the seventeenth century. Few composers did not set it to music. Palestrina has more than thirty settings and Lassus about one hundred.

Musical treatments of this canticle have been extremely varied. Sometimes chanted verses are followed with harmonized plainsong. Often settings are completely original and run the whole gamut of musical expression, from the simplest harmony to the most elaborate dramatic treatment with orchestral accompaniment. A contemporary example would be "Magnificat for a New Millennium" composed by American composer Stephen Perillo. His is a richly sonic setting scored for soloists, chorus, and full orchestra with the addition of glockenspiel, cymbals, drums, bells, triangle, harp, and synthesizer. In it we hear Mary's exuberant gratitude for the inestimable favor bestowed on her by God, for past mercies shown to Israel, and for the fulfillment in the birth of Christ of the promises made to Abraham and to the patriarchs.

For many centuries the social and political significance of the canticle has been virtually bypassed. However, contemporary interpreters point out that, in the *Magnificat*, Mary reveals herself to be as much the disturber of the comfortable as the comforter of the disturbed. Eschewing the role of passive, sweet virgin mother portrayed by Renaissance painters, she vigorously takes up the cause of the poor and the marginalized against the powerful and mighty. With the line "He has shown the strength of his arm: he has scattered the proud in their conceit," she reveals that God will bring about justice for the poor, the abandoned, and those whom society rejects or derides. By her statement that "He has cast down the mighty from their thrones, and has lifted up the lowly," she proclaims that the meek will indeed inherit the earth by possessing the abundance that is their birthright. In this, Mary stands against all forms of domination and discrimination, advocating the reign of mutual respect, equality, and human dignity. She says: "He has filled the hungry with good things, and the rich he has sent away empty," indicating that divine power will be shown in caring for those in need. The prevailing situation, where millions die of starvation while a privileged few hoard the common stock, will and must be corrected.

The accelerated increase in apparitions of Mary during the past five hundred years, beginning with Guadalupe, in Mexico, in 1531, when Mary revealed herself to a poor peasant boy, Juan Diego, makes God's option for the poor and oppressed very clear. Other appearances, in 1830 in Paris, 1858 in Lourdes, 1917 at Fatima, 1945–1959 in Amsterdam, and 1981 in Medjugorje reveal her increasing concern over war, the destruction of nature, the horrors inflicted on so many of God's children by abject poverty and hunger, discrimination, and social injustice.

While listening to the words of the *Magnificat*, one can recall the late medieval picture of Mary the Mother of Mercy holding a cloak over people of every class and kin, initiating a new way of knowing, loving, and acting that has the power to transform the conditions of life on earth.

Mary as Divine Mother

Nothing more is known of Mary's pregnancy until her journey from Nazareth to Judea to be registered for census taking. However, the church honors her, along with the prophets Isaiah and

John the Baptist, as one of the most prominent figures of the Advent liturgy. By Mary's faith and acceptance of God's plans for her, she demonstrates not only her personal joy at the forthcoming birth but also the whole church's expectancy and welcome of Christ.

In the events of Jesus' birth and the Holy Family's subsequent flight into Egypt to escape the threats of King Herod, Mary reveals herself as a physically strong woman of great endurance. She certainly knew very well through personal experience the jealousy, hatred, and venom of the political rulers of her time.

With the Nativity of Christ (celebrated on December 25) the sacred octave of Jesus' life begins to unfold. Mary gives birth to the Christ, the incarnate Son of God, in a lowly stable. Heaven and earth sing praise, the story tells, and Mary "kept all these things, and pondered them in her heart."[6]

The Presentation of Jesus in the Temple and the Purification of Mary (February 2), rites that were Jewish custom forty days after the birth of a male child, is one of the oldest Marian feasts. It was kept in Jerusalem as early as the fourth century and from there was adopted in Constantinople and, by the seventh century, in Rome. The procession traditionally accompanying the festival, in which blessed candles are carried by clergy and worshipers, recalls the manifestation of Christ, the light of the world. Remembered also is Mary and Joseph's bringing of the Holy Child to see the aged Simeon, who had been told that he should not die before he had seen the Lord's Christ. Simeon's response, taking the child in his arms, became the *Nunc Dimittis* canticle sung in Benedictine monasteries each evening during the service of Compline.

*Nunc dimittis servum tuum Domine, secundum verbum
    tuum in pace:
Quia viderunt oculi mei salutare tuum:
Quod parasti ante faciem omnium populorum:
Lumen ad revelationem gentium, et gloriam plebis tuae
    Israel.*

Now Thou dost dismiss Thy servant, O Lord, according
    to Thy word in peace
because my eyes have seen Thy salvation,
which Thou hast prepared before the face of all
    peoples,
a light to the revelation of the Gentiles, and the glory of
    Thy people Israel.[7]

Simeon blesses the infant Jesus and then, addressing Mary directly, prophesies to her saying, "Yea, a sword shall pierce through thy own soul also, that the thoughts of many hearts may be revealed."[8] Through the words of the old man, Mary is made fully aware of the fact that being the mother of Jesus will entail much suffering.

Mary's precise role during the years of Jesus' childhood is not explained in scripture. One can only assume that she was there protecting and nourishing him, as "the child grew and became strong in spirit, filled with wisdom."[9] Certainly the incident during which Mary and Joseph temporarily lose Jesus, only to find him sitting in the temple discoursing with the elder teachers, reveals the very human side of Mary. She hastens to point out to Jesus that she and Joseph have been searching for him, sorrowing, a feeling that all anxious and uncertain parents know.

During the wedding at Cana, when the wine for the guests ran out, Mary perceived the need and pointed it out to her Son, who then performed his first miracle—the changing of water into a wine better than that previously served. This single act has far-reaching symbolic value. Mary comes to the aid of human beings, the guests, by bringing their needs to Christ's attention. The miracle is an acknowledgment of Mary's role as *mediatrix* or mediator, interceding between her Son and the rest of humanity in the reality of their wants and needs.

From this time on, Mary's role is again a silent one until she again appears in the gospel story of the crucifixion. One can surmise that she shared her Son's concerns, moving, as she did, between the roles of mother and disciple. Mary is present at the crucifixion of Jesus. We can identify with the anguish that she must have felt, knowing his innocence and the integrity of his life and message, witnessing how cruelly he was being treated by the jeering crowd. The words from St. John's Gospel, "Now there stood by the cross of Jesus his mother,"[10] rendered in Latin as *Stabat Mater*, best express the pathos of the situation and Mary's deep devotion and faithfulness.

Musical Rendition of the Stabat Mater

The liturgical expression of the *Stabat Mater* is both a hymn and a sequence, or expanded chant. Probably of thirteenth-century Franciscan origin, it was used in the late fifteenth century with the new Mass of the Compassion of the Blessed Virgin Mary. Its present form was not introduced into the Roman Breviary (book accompanying the monastic hours) and Missal (book accompanying the Mass) until 1727:

Stabat Mater dolorosa
  juxta crucem lacrimosa,
  dum pendebat Filius.
Cujus animam gementem,
  contristatam et dolentem,
  pertransivit gladius.
O quam tristis et afflicta
  fuit ilea benedicta
  Mater Unigeniti!
	A weeping Mother was standing
	  full of sorrow beside the cross
	  while her Son was hanging on it.
	Through her grieving soul,
	  anguished and lamenting,
	  a sword had passed.
	O, how sad and afflicted
	  was that blessed Mother
	  of an only Son!

Quail maerebat, et dolebat,
  Pia Mater, dum videbat
  nati poenas inclyti!
Quis est homo qui non fleret
  Christi Matrem si videret
  in tint supplicio?
Quis non pose contristari,
  Christi Matrem contemplari
  dolentem cum Filio?
	She mourned and grieved
	  the Blessed Mother as she saw
	  the suffering of her glorious Son!
	Who is the man who would not weep
	  seeing the Mother of Christ
	  in such torment?
	Who would not feel compassion,
	  watching the Mother of Christ
	  in sorrow with her Son?

Pro peccatis suae gentis
  vidit Jesum in tormentis
  et flagellis subditum.
Vidit suum dulcem Natum
  moriendo desolater
  dum emisit spiritum.
Eja Mater, fons amoris,
  me sentire vim doloris,
  fac, ut tecum lugeam.
	She saw Jesus in torments
	  and subjected to scourging
	  for the sins of his people.
	She saw her dear Son
	  dying forsaken,
	  as he yielded up his spirit.
	O Mother, fount of love,
	  make me feel the strength of thy grief
	  so that I may mourn with thee.

Fac, ut ardeat corn meum
  in amando Christum Deum,
  ut sub complaceam.
Sancta Mater, istud agas:
  crucifixi fige plagas
  cordi meo valide.
Tui Nati vulnerati,
  tam dignati pro me pati,
  poenas mecum divide.
	Make my heart burn
	  with love for Christ my God,
	  so that I may please him.
	Holy Mother, do this for me:
	  fix the wounds of thy crucified Son
	  deeply in my heart.
	Share with me the pains
	  of thy wounded Son
	  who deigned to suffer for me.

Fac me vere tecum flere,	Make me truly weep with thee
crucifixo condolere,	and share the agony of the crucified,
donec ego vixero.	as long as I live.
Juxta crucem tecum stare,	I long to stand with thee beside the cross
et me tibi sociare	and join thee willingly
in planctum desidero.	in thy weeping.
Virgo Virginum praeclara,	O Virgin, peerless among virgins,
mihi jam non sis amara:	do not be harsh towards me,
fac me tecum plangere.	let me weep with thee.
Fac ut portem Christi mortem,	Grant that I may bear Christ's death
passionis fac consortem,	and recall to my mind his fated passion,
et plagas recolere.	and his wounds.
Fac me plagis vulnerari,	Grant that I may be wounded by his wound,
crucem hac inebriari,	intoxicated by his cross,
ob amorem Filii.	for love of thy Son.
Inflammatus et accensus	Inflamed and burning,
per te, Virgo, sim defensus,	may I be defended by thee, O Virgin,
in die judicii.	at the day of judgment.
Fac me cruce custodire,	Grant that I may be protected by the cross,
morte Christi premuniri,	saved by the death of Christ,
confoveri gratia.	and supported by his grace.
Quando corpus morietur,	When my body dies,
fac ut animae donetur	let my soul be granted
paradisi gloria.	the glory of heaven.
Amen.	Amen.

The vivid epic quality and lyricism of the *Stabat Mater* inspired a large number of musical settings before 1700, notably those of Josquin des Prez, Gregor Aichinger, Orlando di Lasso, and Alessandro Scarlatti. Of particular importance is Palestrina's eight-part work, remarkable for its rhythmic fluidity, harmonic expressiveness, and subtle use of varied textures within a double-chorus framework. It is useful to note that these composers, and others to follow, were not working in the monastic or "regular" (inspired by the Rule) tradition. Rather, they were part of the clerical milieu, composing specifically for the church. More will be said on this in chapter 7.

During the eighteenth and nineteenth centuries, many composers gave musical expression to the *Stabat Mater*—Domenico Scarlatti, in the early eighteenth century, employs a tremendous diversity of musical styles to express powerful personal emotions of compassion for the sorrowing Virgin, impassioned desire to share in her grief, and joy at the prospect of joining her Son in heaven. Throughout the work are intermingled examples of the more austere counterpoint of Palestrina, the embellished *bel canto* style, and, at the end, a fugue of great intensity and drama.

One of the most popular settings performed in the modern repertory was composed in 1841 by Gioacchino Rossini. Illustrative of the composer's operatic genius, this rich and elaborate rendition for mixed chorus and orchestra provides an intense musical experience more to be expected in the concert hall than in the church.

Guiseppe Verdi was able, in his *Stabat Mater,* to achieve a deep sincerity of utterance while retaining a style perfected through years of experience with opera. The expressive points are made with great economy and there is no textual repetition. His setting was probably the shortest composed in the nineteenth century, and his example of brevity was followed by a number of other composers. Outstanding settings from the nineteenth and twentieth centuries were composed by Pergolesi, Charpentier, Boccherini, Gounod, Dvořák, Liszt, Kodaly, and Virgil Thomson.

Mary after the Crucifixion

Returning to New Testament references to Mary, one more is found after her appearance at the crucifixion of Jesus. According to the second chapter of the Acts of the Apostles, after Christ's Resurrection and Ascension, Mary went with the apostles into an upper room. They remained there until the day of Pentecost when, with "a sound from heaven, as a mighty wind coming . . . there appeared to them parted tongues as it were of fire, and it sat upon every one of them, and they were all filled with the Holy Spirit" (Acts 2:2–4). From this moment on the apostles were directed to go into all the world to preach the good news of Christ's Resurrection, in essence to create the church. Pope John Paul II points out that Mary's role in this was to be "devoted to prayer" while remaining in their midst.[11] By virtue of this sacred action, Mary is seen as giving birth to the church at Pentecost in the same way as she had given physical birth to its Lord at Bethlehem and to his ministry at Cana. She is the mother not only of Christ but of all believers.

An important Marian feast is the celebration of Mary's Assumption, which takes place on August 15 with an elaborate liturgy and procession. Although the circumstances of Mary's transition from earth to heaven, where and when the event took place, are not known, the church holds that she was taken up, body and soul, into the glory of heaven, and that her mortal body never knew decay. First found in the liturgy of the Eastern Church in the sixth century and represented as the "Dormition," or "going to sleep" rather than the death of the Virgin, the event became a familiar subject of illuminated manuscripts, ivories, and mosaics. At the initiative of Pope Sergius (687–791) the celebration was introduced into the West with the Latin equivalent of the "Dormition of the Virgin." About one hundred years later, its name was changed to "Assumption of the Virgin," indicating a shift of emphasis. Instead of Mary's departure from earthly life, her glorious entry into heaven, welcomed by her Son, became the object of the celebration. It was not until November of 1950, however, that Pope Pius XII removed the Assumption from the realm of popular devotional belief and made it part of the dogma of the church.

The Changing Role of Mary

Across the ages Mary has assumed many roles, reflecting and ennobling believers' highest ideals and aspirations. In the Greco-Roman church of the first two centuries after Christ's birth, the church fathers emphasized Mary's sexual purity and her ability to undo the damage caused the human race by the sin of Eve. Ordinary people saw in her a source of strength and comfort in a society where Christians were the object of persecution.

Once the Emperor Constantine declared freedom of religion for Christians and the church became allied with, rather than repressed by, imperial power, the image of Mary changed again. As Mary was truly the Mother of Jesus, and as Jesus was truly God from the moment of his conception, Mary was seen as the Mother of God as well. The Council of Ephesus in 431 was decisive in clarifying this issue. At that time this truth of the divine motherhood of Mary was solemnly confirmed, to the great joy of Christians. Mary was the *Theotokos* or "God bearer," since by the power of the Holy Spirit she brought into the world Jesus, the Son of God, of one being with the Father.

During the Middle Ages, Mary slowly began to take on some of her Son's functions and was invoked for healing and protection. She was increasingly seen as the fulfillment of biblical prophecies, mediatrix between Christ and his followers. During the tenth to twelfth centuries the word "handmaid" was rarely used, whereas titles of power and majesty abounded. Mary was able to represent believers with her Son, the King, and reconcile them with Him.

In her perceptive book *In Search of Mary*, Sally Cunneen points out new attitudes toward Mary in the writings of Anselm of Canterbury (1033–1109), a Benedictine and church father. Anselm addresses Mary as "Lady" (the feminine equivalent of Lord), letting us understand that in the monastic context she takes the place of the feudal lady so much praised by troubadours and served by knights. In his view, a tender human relationship exists between Jesus and Mary, in heaven and on earth, and the Mother shares with her Son partial responsibility for human salvation. Cunneen goes on to say that:

> Anselm's theology emphasizes the humanity of a Jesus, who is also God, active in the world not only in the past but now. Such a view permeated the entire Church in this monastic era, whose focus on common worship made such connections palpable. As Anselm claimed, the fact that God became human through Mary made people of every degree members of the same family, rooted in a physical creation that was meant to imitate the goodness of God. "As God is the Father of all created things," said Anselm, "so Mary is the Mother of all recreated things, not only human but natural." Central to this two-way traffic between heaven and earth, as Anselm observed, was Mary.[12]

Cunneen quotes from Anselm's *Prayer and Meditations*:

> A woman full and overflowing with grace, plenty flows from you to make all creatures green again. O Virgin blessed and ever blessed, whose blessing is upon all nature, not only is the creature blessed by the Creator, but the Creator is blessed by the creature too.[13]

As already mentioned, one of monasticism's most influential leaders during the twelfth century, a person deeply devoted to the Blessed Virgin, was St. Bernard of Clairvaux (1090–1153). While still a young man, Bernard sought admission to the newly formed monastery of Cîteaux, located in France near Dijon. The purpose of this monastery and the Cistercian Order created there was to restore the Rule of St. Benedict to all of its original discipline and rigor, specifically to correct the perceived artistic and liturgical excesses that had developed through the years at Cluny. In 1115, after only three years at Cîteaux, Bernard was directed to found a new house at Vallée d'Absinthe, or Valley of Bitterness, in the diocese of Langres, a short distance to the north. He renamed the location Claire Vallée or "Clairvaux" and from then on his name was inseparably associated with this monastery.

Known for his magnetic rhetoric and his enthusiasm and fervor in promoting Cistercian ideals, Bernard had a tremendous impact on the religious and political life of his time. His energetic impulse led to the creation of more than three hundred Cistercian daughter houses in England and across Western Europe to Russia. Although his writings on the Blessed Virgin were not extensive—he felt that all language failed before her incomprehensible glory!—he is credited more than anyone else in the creation of the twelfth-century cult of the Virgin.

In the thirteenth century, the kingdom of France was governed on two occasions with wisdom and firmness by Blanche de Castille, queen of the deceased Louis VIII and mother of the future Louis IX, who was to become Saint Louis. The devotion of the young king to Christ and his mother, as well as to his own mother, was a powerful element in spreading devotion to "Our Lady," whose cathedrals covered the kingdom "as a white robe." Numerous images of the Coronation of the Virgin by her Son, donated by Blanche and Louis, grace the cathedrals of France, and the rose window of the north transept of Chartres Cathedral is also their gift.

One of the most significant medieval portrayals of the Blessed Mother is that of *Sedes Sapientiae* or "Seat of Wisdom," examples of which are to be found sculpted on the western portals of many French cathedrals of the time or painted in their stained glass windows. The pose is hieratic—on her lap the seated Virgin provides a seat for Christ, the embodiment of the wisdom of God. She grounds and provides a place for wisdom to play and interact with creation.

So widespread was devotion to Mary during the twelfth and thirteenth centuries that nearly all the cathedrals of Western Europe built at that time are dedicated to *Notre Dame*, "Our Lady." Their stained glass windows and sculptures reveal every form of nature—flowers, plants, animals—and every kind of craftsman and worker, male and female—farmers, spinners, weavers, vintners, and furriers. Mary's sphere of influence was vast. She was the link between humanity and God. Her images—seated with a book awaiting the Annunciation, the Annunciation itself, the Visitation, the Presentation at the Temple, the Coronation by Christ—are approachable yet never sentimental; they are engaging and human, yet invite the mind to contemplate an inner reality, illumined by divine light.

The Byzantine Akathistos Hymn of the Feast of the Annunciation, (named *a-cathistos*, "not sitting," since it was traditionally sung standing), the most ancient Marian hymn of all Christian literature, explains Mary's power to interpret the wisdom of God through her own radiant understanding:

> Rejoice, vessel of the Wisdom of God, storehouse for his providence.
> Rejoice, for philosophers are revealed as fools, the logic of logicians is dislodged.
> Rejoice, for keen disputants grow dull, the makers of myths run dry.
> Rejoice, so you break the Athenian web, and fill full the nets of the fishermen.
> Rejoice, for you draw souls from the depths of unknowing and bathe them in light that contains all knowledge.[14]

The Marian Anthems

During the twelfth and thirteenth centuries, many churches adopted the practice of singing older antiphons to the Blessed Virgin Mary as devotional acts in themselves, not connected to psalmody. Four of these antiphons are of great beauty and importance and have played a prominent role in the development of polyphonic compositions: the *Alma Redemptoris Mater*, "Gracious Mother of the Redeemer," the *Ave Regina Caelorum*, "Hail,

Queen of the Heavens," the *Regina Caeli*, "Rejoice, Queen of the Heavens," and the *Salve Regina*, "Hail, O Queen."

Here we may note that the word "anthem" is an English corruption of the Late Latin word *antiphona*, shortened to *antiphon*. Before the Reformation, it was used chiefly to designate independent chants, such as the Marian antiphons, both in their monophonic and polyphonic settings. This is probably why the *Liber Usualis* with English rubrics calls the Marian antiphons "Anthems to the Blessed Virgin Mary." By extension of usage, the word "anthem" came to mean any sacred, vocal composition.

In the year 1239, Pope Gregory IX ordered that, according to season, one of the four Marian anthems be sung at the end of Compline. The Alma Redemptoris Mater, which enjoyed the greatest popularity in the later Middle Ages, was sung from the beginning of Advent through February 1. The composition of this hymn is often credited to Swiss-born Benedictine monk Hermann Contractus (1013–1054), chronicler, mathematician, musician, and poet. A cripple from birth (hence the name "Contractus"), he was unable to move without assistance but his great determination helped him to overcome all obstacles so that he became a shining light in the most diversified branches of learning—theology, mathematics, astronomy, music, and the Latin, Greek, and Arabic languages. Students flocked to him from all over Europe, attracted not only by his outstanding scholarship but also by his monastic virtues and his lovable personality. A monument to his great industry and outstanding erudition is his chronicle of the most important events from the birth of Christ to his day.

Pope John Paul II, in his 1987 encyclical, invited us to reflect on the words of Hermann Contractus's anthem and to sing them in anticipation of the turn of the millennium. In the wake of the World Trade Center disaster, their message is even more poignant.

Alma Redemptoris Mater, quae pervia caeli porta manes,
Et stella maris, succurre cadenti surgere qui curat populo:
Tu quae genital, natura mirante, tuum sanctum Genitorem:
Virgo prius ac posterius, Gabrielis ab ore sumens illud Ave,
    peccatorum miserere.

O loving Mother of our Redeemer, gate of heaven, star
    of the sea,
Hasten to aid thy fallen people who strive to rise once more.
Thou who brought forth thy holy Creator, all creation
    wond'ring,
Yet remainest ever Virgin, taking from Gabriel's lips
    that joyful "Hail!": be merciful to us sinners.

The pope reflects that these words express the truth of the "great transformation" that the mystery of the Incarnation establishes for human beings:

It is an unending and continuous transformation between falling and rising again, between the person of sin and the person of grace and justice...Year after year the antiphon rises to Mary, evoking that moment which saw the accomplishment of this essential historical transformation, which irreversibly continues, the transformation from "falling" to "rising."[15]

The Ave Regina Caelorum, preferred along with the Salve Regina by Renaissance composers, was sung from February 2 through Wednesday of Holy Week. This is a processional antiphon and, despite its use during Lent, repeatedly greets Mary in words that express joy and confidence in her intercession. Mary is Queen, Lady, root, and gate. She is greeted with expressions of increasing intensity that English translation does not sufficiently render: *Ave, Salve, Gaude, Vale*. These are forms of greeting, acclamations that show augmented intensity and regard.

> *Ave Regina caelorum, Ave Domina Angelorum:*
> *Salve radix, salve porta, Ex qua mundo lux est orta:*
> *Gaude, Virgo gloriosa, Super omnes speciosa:*
> *Vale, o valde decora, Et pro nobis Christum exora.*

> Welcome, O queen of Heaven. Welcome, O Lady of
>   Angels.
> Hail! thou root, hail! thou gate from whom unto the
>   world, a light has arisen.
> Rejoice, O glorious Virgin, lovely beyond all others,
> Farewell, most beautiful maiden, and pray for us to
>   Christ.

From the fifteenth century on, the Ave Regina Caelorum text lent itself to a great variety of musical interpretations, notably from composers Guillaume Dufay (d. 1474) and Tomas Luis de Victoria (1548–1611). In the eighteenth century Joseph Haydn also created a powerful setting.

The Regina Caeli, Eastertide anthem of the Blessed Virgin Mary, celebrates the joy of Christ's Resurrection and appears in the liturgy from Holy Saturday, the day before Easter, until the week after Pentecost. Of unknown authorship, this anthem has ancient origins. Legend says that St. Gregory the Great heard the first three lines chanted by angels on a certain Easter morning in Rome while he walked barefoot in a great religious procession and promptly added the line "*Ora pro nobis Deum, alleluia.*"

Regina caeli, laetare, alleluia;
Quia quem meruisti portare, alleluia.
Resurrexit sicut dixit, alleluia:
Ora pro nobis Deum, alleluia.
Gaude et laetare, Virgo Maria, alleluia.
Quia surrexit Dominus vere, alleluia.

Queen of heaven, rejoice, alleluia!
For He whom thou didst merit to bear, alleluia
Hath risen, as He said, alleluia;
Pray for us to God, alleluia.
Rejoice and be glad, O Virgin Mary, alleluia.
Because the Lord is truly risen, alleluia.

The plainchant prayer form is used on weekdays during the Easter season. For the Easter celebration itself, the later musical forms of polyphonic and ornate styles are used. The chant gives a sense of joy and delight, the joy of the Resurrection resounding after the heavy season of Lent. Among many famous composers who set this anthem to music are W. A. Mozart and Leoncavallo in the Easter procession of his opera *Cavalleria Rusticana*. The antiphon is sung in several variations today.

The Salve Regina, particularly beloved of the monastic community, was chanted from the week after Pentecost until Advent as a final salute to Our Lady at the close of the day. It was popular as evening song at medieval universities and was the frequent setting for the devotion known as Benediction of the Blessed Sacrament. It was well known and established in France and Germany by the twelfth century, and was part of the liturgical prayer of many religious orders.

The fact that the plainchant versions of the Salve Regina were so familiar and so much loved may have contributed to the fact that relatively few musical settings (in comparison to those of the Regina Caeli, for instance) became popular for liturgical use. The plainchant Salve, unlike the other antiphons, can be found in troped versions, where expanded text is intermingled with the original base text. Examples of the use of *Salve Regina* as a hymn are found in every period: Johannes Ockeghem (d. 1496?), Orlando di Lasso (d. 1594), Joseph Haydn (d. 1809), and Marcel Dupré (d. 1971). Here is the text:

> *Salve, Regina, mater misericordiae: Vita, dulcedo, et spes nostra, salve.*
> *Ad te clamamus, exsules, filii Hevae.*
> *Ad te suspiramus, gementes et flentes in hac lacrimarum valle.*
> *Eia ergo, Advocata nostra, illos tuos misericordes oculos ad nos converte.*
> *Et Jesum, benedictum fructum ventris tui, nobis post hoc exsilium ostende.*
> *O clemens: O pia: O dulcis Virgo Maria*

> Hail Queen, mother of mercy, sweetness in life and our hope, hail.
> Exiled children of Eve, we cry out to you,
> we sigh to you, groaning and weeping in this vale of tears.
> Then come now, our advocate, turn your merciful eyes towards us,

and show us Jesus, the blessed fruit of your womb, after
    this time of our exile,
O forgiving one, O pious one, O sweet Virgin Mary.

These Marian anthems differ considerably from the older,
very brief Office antiphons. Their texts are longer and they are
given more elaborate settings with wider ranges and even occa-
sional melismas. These texts also served as the basis for many
polyphonic masses.

It has been calculated that there exist some fifteen thousand
hymns in honor of Our Lady. Around four thousand are origi-
nals, while the others derive from them in one way or another.
One of the most beloved, Ave Maris Stella, has been translated
by Fr. Ralph Wright, O.S.B., of the Abbey of St. Mary and St.
Louis, St. Louis, Missouri:

EXAMPLE 1: AVE MARIS STELLA

AVE MARIS STELLA

Star of sea and ocean,
Gateway to Man's haven,
Mother of our Maker,
Hear our prayer, O maiden.

Welcoming the Ave
Of God's simple greeting,
You have borne a Saviour
Far beyond all dreaming.

Gentlest of all virgins,
That our love be faithful,
Keep us from all evil,
Gentle, strong and grateful.

Loose the bonds that hold us
Bound in sin's own blindness,
That with eyes now opened,
God's own light may guide us.

Show yourself, our Mother:
He will hear your pleading
Whom your womb has sheltered
And whose hands bring healing.

Guard us through life's dangers,
Never turn and leave us,
May our hope find harbour
In the calm of Jesus.

Sing to God our Father
Through the Son who saves us;
Joyful in the Spirit
Everlasting praises.

Text: Ralph Wright, O.S.B., from *Ave Maris Stella* (8th century). Tune: C. Ett, Cantica Sacra, 1840. Appearing in *Hymns for Prayer and Praise* (Chicago, Ill.: GIA Publications Inc., 1989). Used with permission.

7
The Elaboration and Vertical Expansion of Chant

"Give glory to God's own name."
St. Benedict

During the ninth to the twelfth centuries, abbeys and monasteries nurtured music theory and practice. The chant repertory, grown extremely stylized and sophisticated under the influence of Charlemagne, spread far across Europe by the crisscrossing back and forth of lines of communication between the great monastic houses. An elaborate "interlibrary loan system" between monasteries ensured that liturgical books, many of which contained precious examples of chant, were available for use and for copying.

Within the monasteries themselves, classical treatises on music were preserved along with practical musical sources. The ninth-century library at Reichenau (located in southwestern Germany, near Lake Constance) retained copies of works on music by Augustine, Isidore, Cassiodorus, and Boethius in addition to ten antiphonaries containing music for the Opus Dei. The Abbey of St. Gall, nearby in Switzerland, had a very active musical scriptorium that produced a large number of chant manuscripts in its own distinctive musical script; and the Monastery of St. Martial in Limoges, France, possessed a rich collection of manuscripts illustrating musical additions to the liturgy dating from the tenth to the twelfth centuries.

Other significant sources of medieval music survive from Santiago de Compostela (the *Codex Calixtinus* containing music brought by pilgrims to the shrine of St. James), from St. Denis, a royal abbey in northern France, and from Las Huelgas, a women's convent in Spain that had a flourishing choir school. Most monasteries held in their possession at least a few choir books with chants for either Mass or Office.

During these centuries when Benedictine influence was at its zenith, musical developments in Western Europe were almost entirely carried out by monastic composers working in a liturgical context. At first the focus of attention was not on the Ordinary of the Mass—the *Kyrie*, *Gloria*, *Credo*, *Sanctus*, and *Agnus Dei*—as has been the case from the Renaissance to our own day, but rather on the Propers—the *Introit*, *Gradual*, *Alleluia*, *Offertory*, and *Communion*. As already explained, the *Gradual*, the *Alleluia*, and the *Tract* were sung at moments of reflection between the scriptural readings, times during which celebrant and congregation were not actively engaged in responsorial exchange, and the *Offertory* and the *Communion* also provided "waiting time" while the gifts were presented and communion was received. Monastic composers saw these as precious moments for exercising their creative energies.

Troping

A very important form of music elaboration was "troping," the addition of new textual or musical material to a pre-existent liturgical chant. The chief function of troping was to explain or enlarge upon the meaning of the official liturgical text. Tropes might also establish additional connections between the text and a particular day or season of the liturgical year. They served to emphasize the solemnity and significance of certain feasts or holy days.

Before Carolingian times, none of the parts of the Ordinary —which had come from the Eastern Church—had a Gregorian melody. Since they were sung responsively by the celebrant and the congregation and not given a special setting to be sung by the *schola*, they never received an artistic setting within the Gregorian repertory. However, they did eventually attract the attention of Frankish composers and began, also, to be frequently troped.

The new phrases of text and music were added before the chant line or at the end, or even inserted between its phrases. Generally the tropes were freely composed in the style of the original chant melody, but related to it only by unity of mode and smooth connections between the old and new phrases. Many tropes were far longer than the official chant, which gave the whole melody the impression of being no more than a series of familiar quotations inserted in a new and otherwise original piece of music—a result not entirely pleasing to advocates of the traditional liturgy.

In the following example, the trope, *Celestium terrestrium et infernorum rex*, "King of the heavens, the earth, and the lower regions" has been placed between the words of the *Gloria*, represented in capital letters:

EXAMPLE 1: GLORIA TROPE

QUONI-AM TU SOLUS SANCTUS. TU SOLUS DOMINUS.

Ce-les-ti-um terres-tri-um et infer-no-rum rex.

TU SOLUS ALTISSIMUS.

FOR THOU ONLY ART HOLY, THOU ONLY ART THE LORD. King of the heavens, the earth, and the lower regions. THOU ALONE ART THE MOST HIGH.

From David Hiley, *Western Plainchant* (Oxford, England: Clarendon Press, 1993), 208.

The way that the presence of tropes extended the worship service was ill-suited to the parish church but flourished in monasteries, where sung services often occupied as much as eight to twelve hours of the day. In this milieu, the composition of tropes attracted the most intelligent and gifted talent of the time.

Sequences

Legend has it that a Benedictine monk of the monastery of St. Gall, Notker Balbulus (Notker the Stutterer, 840–912) is credited with the invention of another musical innovation. Famous in his day as a teacher, a poet, and the author of a prose account of the deeds of Charlemagne, Notker tells a story of his involvement in the writing of "sequences"—tropes that took on a life of their own, becoming separate pieces independent of the chant to which they had been attached.

When Notker was a youth he found it hard to remember the extremely long melismatic melodies that prolonged the final "a" of the *Alleluia* of the Mass and wished for some device to aid his "unstable little memory." One day a monk from Jumièges near Rouen arrived at St. Gall after his own monastery had been ravaged by the Normans. He brought with him an antiphonary in which each note of the *Alleluia* trope corresponded to a syllable of text. The idea delighted Notker so much that he began to write words himself. Through his efforts and those of others, the sequence was born.

At first, the sequence was a type of trope often attached to the *Alleluia* as amplification. Soon, however, it became an elaborate new composition capable of standing on its own. The new sequences made frequent use of paired lines of equal length and even of rhyme, so that gradually they became more poetic in style. Traditionally these innovative pieces were sung by the *schola* just before the gospel reading of the Mass. The fact that some 4,500 sequences were composed during the Middle Ages and early Renaissance indicates the enthusiasm with which monastic writers and composers seized this opportunity for enrichment of the liturgy.

Addition of Feast Days

Beginning in the ninth century there was a tremendous growth in the number of feast days or religious festivals. Most of the new feasts honored individual saints, particularly the Virgin Mary, but medieval religious composers also made additions to the schedule of regular yearly services, such as Trinity Sunday, Corpus Christi, and All Souls'. Each new feast required a Mass and a complete set of services for all the hours. Visiting the resting place of the complete body of an important saint might be the goal of pilgrims, as happened when the body of St. James was translated to Santiago de Compostela in northwestern Spain. Whenever physical remains or relics of a saint were present, there was a more solemn celebration of his or her feast occasioning more new music.

Hymns

Within the context of the monastery, the hymn was the most elegant expression of newer, more poetic innovations. It showed regularity in the number of syllables in each line and the number of lines in each repeated verse or strophe. The hymn's melody was constructed in a very organized, regular pattern with a strong cadence or feeling of closure after every second line. Weaker cadences were used at the ends of odd-numbered lines. Over time there were more and more examples where two lines belonging together (couplets) were made to rhyme and rhyming lines of the same number of syllables were given identical stress patterns.

The Abbey of St. Martial of Limoges, famous for its tropes and sequences, also possessed one of the most important collections of this new rhythmic poetry, dating from around 1050 to 1150.

Liturgical Drama

Like the sequence, the liturgical drama began as a trope of chant. One of the earliest recorded versions depicts the encounter of the three Marys with an angel at the tomb of Christ on Easter morning. Named from its beginning words, *"Quem quaeritis?"* ("Whom are ye seeking?"), the "play" consists of only three lines of dialogue. This Easter play served as a model for various Christmas plays that might also include elaborate scenes at King Herod's court, the slaughter of the innocents, and the lament of Rachel.

The play of Daniel, written at Beauvais in northern France in about 1150, with solos and choruses, is the most spectacular of these plays. Its speeches, with few exceptions, are rhymed and use metrical verses similar to those of contemporary hymns and sequences. Much of the dramatic substance and brilliance of Daniel resided in the pageantry accompanied by processional songs called "conducti," which were processionals to conduct someone—king, queen, or Daniel—on or off the scene.

Other plays were dramatized stories from the Old and New Testaments, and a few are not biblical at all, but are devoted to the much appreciated miracles of St. Nicholas. The liturgical dramas were always sung in Latin, with single-line melodies, often retaining the character of chant.

If Hildegard of Bingen's *Ordo Virtutum* may be taken as example, we can assume that a number of early religious dramas were created by monastics. However, after the year 1300, religious plays were more often composed by church musicians, presented in the vernacular language of the people, and performed in the parvis or space in front of the main church door. Called miracle plays, they portrayed stories of the Virgin Mary or the saints and also stories taken from the Bible. The actors were often laypeople who were not trained singers.

A larger step away from the monasteries but still based on the rhyming Latin chant of the 1100s was the work of the troubadours, composers of secular poems and music at the brilliant courts of Provence in southern France. They and their northern French counterparts, the *trouvères*, turned chant-inspired melodies into songs of courtly love.

From the 1100s on, the single melodic line of the chant was applied in ever-widening geographical and social circles. Eventually it became folk song and, with its rhymed strophic form, inspired dance music such as the ballade, the lai, and the rondeau.

This musical activity was taking place at a time when the Crusades were bringing into contact—frequently violent contact—peoples of East and West. Returning Crusaders brought back memories filled with wonders they had seen in the East, not only majestic architecture, mosaics, and relics but also, no doubt, the sound of songs and music. It is therefore not surprising that many of these compositions have a decidedly oriental sound.

Vocal Polyphony

Concurrent with all the embellishments to the chant, there arose another means of increasing the splendor and solemnity of the liturgy. This development, called "polyphony" (music of many voices) can be regarded as a kind of trope in which new notes appeared together with the chant, forming harmonies, rather than being added to it by monophonic extension. As church architecture gradually moved from the earth-bound Romanesque toward the soaring Gothic, Western music took on a vertical dimension that has been its hallmark ever since. The distance between a polyphonic work of the late twelfth century and one of our day may seem immense, but the latter could never have been written without the development of the former, which used Gregorian chant as its base. To make this clear, we will now speak specifically about the history of Western religious music as it developed out of the early chant.

One of the earliest music theorists to explain the phenomenon of polyphony was a Benedictine monk, Hucbald of St. Amand (840–930). Hucbald is credited with authorship of two of the most important musical treatises of the time, the *Musica enchiriadis* (Music Manual) and the *Scholia enchiriadis* (Commentary on the Manual). In these books, Hucbald explains how to sing in parallel with a chant, above or below, at an interval of an octave (*Do* with the *Do* above), a fourth (*Do* with the *Sol* below or the *Fa* above), or a fifth (*Do* with the *Fa* below or the *Sol* above). This harmonious mixture of two tones, produced from different sources and meeting in one joined sound, he referred to as "organum."

For the singers, organum meant singing the same chant, but part of the group would start a fourth, fifth, or octave away from the normal pitch. For the listeners, the result was a series of very resonant sonorities with a single melodic profile, that of the original chant. This is called "parallel organum."

Examples 2 and 3 illustrate parallel organum at the octave and at the fifth.

EXAMPLE 2: PARALLEL ORGANUM AT THE OCTAVE ABOVE AND BELOW

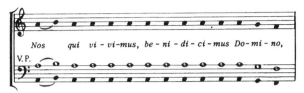

We who are living will bless the Lord from this time forth and forever (Ps 115:18).

From Richard H. Hoppin, *Medieval Music* (New York: W. W. Norton & Company, 1978), 190.

EXAMPLE 3: THREE FORMS OF PARALLEL ORGANUM AT THE FIFTH

From Richard H. Hoppin, *Medieval Music* (New York: W. W. Norton & Company, 1978), 190.

A somewhat different sound could be created by starting both parts on the same pitch and having one voice hold steady while the other moved up or down until the fourth or fifth was reached and then continuing in parallel motion.

EXAMPLE 4: MODIFIED PARALLEL ORGANUM

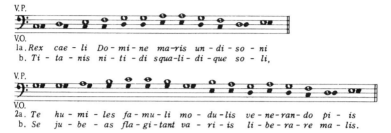

V.P.

V.O.
1a. *Rex   cae - li   Do - mi - ne   ma-ris   un - di - so - ni*
 b. *Ti - ta - nis   ni - ti - di squa-li - di -que   so - li,*

V.P.

V.O.
2a. *Te   hu - mi - les   fa - mu - li   mo - du -lis   ve - ne - ran- do   pi - is*
 b. *Se   ju - be - as   fla - gi - tant va - ri - is   li - be - ra - re   ma - lis.*

King of Heaven, Lord of the roaring sea, of the shining sun and the dark earth, Thy humble servants, by worshiping with pious melodies, beg you to free them from diverse ills.

From Richard H. Hoppin, *Medieval Music* (New York: W. W. Norton & Company, 1978), 191.

In these early organa the chant itself was known as the *cantus firmus* and the additional voice providing the harmony as the organal voice. As time went on, the organal voice became much more daring, choosing its tones independently of the melody below it, although the two voices were still sounded at the same time with the same rhythm. Notice, in Example 5, the variety of intervals allowed here, some in even wider-than-octave range.

In melismatic organum, note-against-note writing almost disappears and we find an organal voice with several or many notes against each note of the chant. The *cantus firmus* is slowed down, sounded in long drawn-out tones, while the added voice runs above it in an elaborate series of much shorter notes. The overall effect is one of lightness and delicacy in the upper voice and strength and solidity in the lower. In this one is reminded of the elaborate tracery in the upper parts of the windows of the great gothic cathedrals contrasting with the solidity of their pier buttresses. Example 6 illustrates St. Martial Melismatic Organum.

EXAMPLE 5: FREE ORGANUM OF THE 11TH CENTURY

All powerful creator God, have mercy. Christ, splendor of God, virtue and wisdom of the Father, have mercy. Sacred breath, bond, and love of both, have mercy.

From Archibald T. Davison and Willi Apel, *Historical Anthology of Music*, rev. ed. (Cambridge, Mass.: Harvard University Press, 1976), 22. Used with permission.

EXAMPLE 6: ST. MARTIAL MELISMATIC ORGANUM

Pray for us.

From Richard H. Hoppin, *Medieval Music* (New York: W. W. Norton & Company, 1978), 202.

At the beginning of the twelfth century, vocal polyphony, the subject of much experimentation, was an established partner with Gregorian chant, both serving to add splendor to the liturgical celebration. Almost all of the new material—both literary and musical—was of monastic origin. Poems and melodies composed by monks became the common fund of the universal liturgy, arising from such renowned abbeys as St. Gall, Fleury, Montecassino, and St. Martial.

Whereas the essential elements of the Mass and the Opus Dei had been settled before the Carolingian monastic revival at the end of the eighth century, it was during the ninth to the twelfth centuries that the minor texts were established. These included the formulas for the benediction or blessing of the lessons, the absolutions (remission of sins), and all the accessory pieces that enriched the primary texts. The liturgy was never considered a complete and final whole to which nothing further might be added, and monks and nuns saw it as a stimulus to and outcome of their creative activity.

Monastic and Secular Schools

It is important to mention a development in medieval Christianity which, although begun in prior centuries, came to the fore in the twelfth century. This was the development of two different types of schools, each with its own purpose and milieu.

The first type of school was the monastic school, which was open to boys who were destined for the monastic life. These young monks received training individually under the guidance of an abbot through reading the Bible and the church fathers within the framework of monastic life. Their focus was not so much to gain speculative insights as it was to savor and cling to the search for God.

The other type of school, external rather than internal in emphasis, was the clerical school. Clerical schools were situated near cathedrals, in the cities and often outside the cloister walls. They were attended by young men who were preparing for pastoral activity, for the active rather than the contemplative Christian life.

Whereas both types of schools espoused the same theology, the approach to it was completely different. Following St. Gregory's description of St. Benedict as *scienter nescius et sapienter indoctus* ("learnedly ignorant and wisely unlearned"), monastics made reverence for God's mysteries, experienced in the life of prayer, their first priority.[1] Not wishing to be distracted by numerous and superfluous problems posed by the intellect, they depended on their own direct experience. They sought not so much to reveal the mysteries of God, to explicate them or derive from them any speculative conclusions, but to fill their whole lives with them.

The teachers and students of clerical schools, soon to be referred to as "scholastics," were concerned, on the other hand, with achieving clarity through use of the intellect. Rather than referring back to tradition, they favored pursuit of problems and finding new solutions. Their purpose was to remove subjective or experiential material from Christian teachings so as to make them as rational and scientific as possible.

These two schools gave rise to different types of religious, the "regular" clergy (from Latin *regula*, "rule") who belonged to religious orders and were bound by their rules, and the secular clergy, those who did not. In this context, the word "secular" does not mean "temporal" as opposed to spiritual. The secular clergy were responsible for the life of the church, rather than the monastery, and the pastoral care of its believers.

During the twelfth century monasticism reached its zenith. It then began slowly to withdraw from the musical scene as attention shifted to the developing secular schools, to their off-shoots, the universities, and to the brilliant musical life created in the churches and later in the royal courts. With the develop-ment of vocal polyphony, Gregorian chant had less influence. Gone forever were the conditions where one part was the whole. The freedom of the single line and the elegant simplicity of up and down retreated behind monastery walls as its more complex musical offspring took center stage.

The School of Notre Dame

Two French composers, Léonin (1159–1201) and Pérotin (1170–1236) and their associates were leading exponents of the new church music based on Gregorian chant but revealing some dar-ing innovations. Both were connected with the Paris cathedral of Notre Dame and both achieved significant advances in the development of music sung in parts.

Léonin is well-known for two styles: the discant or note-against-note style, where the lower voice moves as fast or almost as fast as the upper voice, and the regular organum, where the ratio of the number of notes in the upper part to that in the lower is often very high—as many as thirty or forty to one!

EXAMPLE 7: LÉONIN, ORGANUM DUPLUM

Alleluia

From Donald J. Grout and Claude V. Palisca, *A History of Western Music* (New York: W. W. Norton & Company, 1996), 82.

For the first time, specific rhythmical patterns were introduced based, perhaps, on the meter of French and Latin verse. The basic patterns were codified as the six rhythmic modes:[2]

EXAMPLE 8: RHYTHMIC MODES

Mode	Musical equivalent
1	♩ ♪
2	♪ ♩
3	♩. ♪ ♩
4	♪ ♩ ♩.
5	♩. ♩.
6	♫♪

In the discant, the upper voice became more and more melodic. Its longs and shorts were measured to the accompanying notes of the lower voice, which was perceived to march along in equal units. Although the basic sound was consonant—unisons, fourths, and fifths were the stable harmonies—partial dissonances were also included, especially the third (*Do* to *Mi*). In the following example, taken from St. Martial but illustrating the discant style, note that contrary motion, one part descending while the other ascends, is also used:

EXAMPLE 9: VERSUS IN DISCANT STYLE, SCHOOL OF ST. MARTIAL

O-mnis cu - ret ho - mo pro-me - re can - ti   -   ca   Sunt com-ple - ta mo-do

di - cta   pro - phe   -   ti   -   -   -   -   ca.

Let every man take care to pour forth songs; the prophetic sayings are now fulfilled.

Richard H. Hoppin, editor, *Anthology of Medieval Music* (New York: W. W. Norton & Company, 1978), 44.

Since Léonin was writing basically for the Mass, we can imagine an occasion celebrated in high solemnity and sung mostly in

chant up to the *Gradual* where, in place of the expected Gregorian, worshipers heard the cantor's rendition of an extraordinary
flight of ornamentation over the drastically slowed down chant.
These extremely melismatic organa would have alternated with
animated discant at irregular intervals just to keep everyone alert!

The most important innovation made by Léonin's successor,
Pérotin, was the expansion of polyphony to two, three, and even
four voices. In these compositions the *cantus firmus* is called the
"tenor" (from Latin *tenere*, "to hold," because of the way it main-
tains the chant notes). The "duplum" is the voice next above the
tenor and the "triplum" is the voice above that. In the example
given here, the two upper voices move in measured phrases above
the long-held notes in the tenor. Notice that the voices sometimes cross so that the triplum sounds lower than the duplum.

EXAMPLE 10: ORGANA TRIPLA

From Richard H. Hoppin, *Medieval Music* (New York, W. W. Norton & Company,
1978), 237.

The need to coordinate and organize these two or even three voices above the tenor accounts for the change away from elaborate melismas toward shorter and more regular phrases. Interest shifts away from the melody to rhythmic and chordal structure.

We need to remember that medieval polyphony was largely designed for a small ensemble of expert soloists, well trained in improvisation and capable of great vocal virtuosity. Today, on the contrary, we expect polyphony to be sung by large choral groups and think of solo song as a soloist's melody against a harmonic background.

Medieval musicians delighted in composing elaborate conducti to be used to honor saints, mark the coronation of kings and the consecration of bishops, or welcome special visitors. In these the tenor was often not taken from chant but was an original, newly composed melody. Most probably these conducti used instruments as well as voices for many of the parts.

The Motet

A natural development in polyphonic writing was the "motet" (from French *mot*, "word"), essentially a literary activity, where the upper, melismatic voices of the organum were given words that troped the text of the plainchant tenor (see Example 11).

Untroubled by the singing together of two or more different sets of words, the medieval composers carried the process several steps further: French texts, usually secular in content, were added in the upper parts. Motets gradually lost any connection with Gregorian chant and became songs of courtly love rather than religious devotion. The tenor line may have been an instrumental rather than a vocal line.

EXAMPLE 11: MOTET ATTRIBUTED TO FRANCO OF COLOGNE (CA. 1260)
PSALLAT CHORUS/EXIMIE/APTATUR

Triplum: *Let the choir sing a new song with tuneful melody in Thy name, O great Father.*

Duplum: *O excellent and regal father, O pious ruler, O outstanding teacher, pray today to Jesus, the Son of Mary.*

Tenor   *. . . is prepared . . .*

From *The Oxford Anthology of Music: Medieval Music*, edited by W. Thomas Marrocco and Nicholas Sandon (London: Oxford University Press, 1977), 104. Used with permission.

The Ars Nova *or New Art*

During the fourteenth century the motet continued to become increasingly secularized. Fidelity to the liturgical text of the old *cantus firmus* was left behind as devotion often yielded to the demands of art. The different parts not only carried entirely different words; they often were sung in canonic form, where all the voices sang the same melody but would not begin at the same time. Popular as well was the use of a technique known as "hocket" (from French *hoquet*, "hiccup") in which one voice sings while the other is silent. The following example shows how the upper parts often alternated single notes, each voice filling in the rests of the other:

EXAMPLE 12: HOCKET

Triplum: For in her nothing is lacking. Duplum: [This] my heart knows, which feels it.

From Richard H. Hoppin, *Medieval Music* (New York: W. W. Norton & Company, 1978), 345.

French composer Philippe de Vitry dubbed the new innovative music *Ars Nova*, or "New Art." His motets added a fourth voice called the "contra tenor," which moved in the same range and with the same note values as the tenor but which added complexity to the basic shape of the composition. Chords expanded beyond the limits of an octave and the rhythmical relationship of the parts to each other became much more precise.

The most famous fourteenth-century *Ars Nova* composer was Guillaume de Machaut (1300–1377). Known particularly for composing two-part secular songs, an elaboration on the work of the *trouvères*, Machaut nevertheless composed his most important work using a liturgical subject, the Ordinary of the Mass. This *Messe de Notre Dame* is the first illustration of a Mass composed as one piece of music, with a uniform style and recurring melodic elements.

Ars Nova continued the shift from sacred to secular composition. In Italy three new forms appeared, all owing a debt to these French compositions: the early madrigal, two voices set to pastoral or vernacular poetry; the *ballata*, a song to accompany dancing; and the *caccia* (Fr. *chasse*, "chase"), where a popular-style melody was set in strict canon to lively, graphically descriptive words. The name refers not just to the pursuit of one voice after the other but also to the subject matter, which often described a hunt or some other animated scene such as a bustling marketplace, a fair, or a battle. Vivid details are brought out with spirited humor in the music, often with hocket and echo effects.

Throughout the fourteenth century new rhythmic freedom was introduced, sometimes to almost unperformable extremes. The counterpoint or combining of melodic lines, note for note, was further perfected, with better balance between perfect consonances (fifths and octaves), imperfect ones (thirds and sixths), and some dissonances. Composers aimed to achieve a pleasing, attractive sound.

Fifteenth Century Developments

During the 1400s, Gregorian chant was still strongly favored as a compositional starting point. Polyphonic music gained a more international flavor with important innovations taking place in the north of France, in Flanders (modern day Belgium and Holland, along the North Sea), and in England.

Drawing melodies both from chant and popular song, Flem-
ish composers created very demanding forms of the Mass and the
motet. Four-part polyphony became a basic minimum and composers sometimes used eight, sixteen, or even more parts. The
melody line was manipulated by stretching it out with notes of
longer duration or by diminution, giving it notes of shorter time
value. It could be played or sung backward in another voice; it
could also be turned upside down upon repetition, so that if the
principal melody jumps upward by so many steps, the tones of
the counter melody or of the other parts move downward by the
same number of steps, creating a mirror image.

The leading English composer, John Dunstable (ca. 1390–
1453), became known for the creation of "song motets"—small
devotional pieces sung after Mass or Vespers. These post-liturgi-
cal devotions became increasingly popular during the 1400s.
Dunstable sometimes used the familiar chant associated with the
text not as tenor *cantus firmus* but rather as a paraphrased top
part with a new rhythm and added ornamentation. Dunstable
began to group Mass pieces in pairs, a *Gloria* with a *Credo*, a
Sanctus with an *Agnus Dei*, in which case one or the other had
to forego its own appropriate chant as *cantus firmus*.

English composers devised a technique of improvisation,
called "faburden," or "false drone," which consisted of placing
parallel thirds above the chant and, at the same time, parallel
fourths below, making sixths sounding together (see Example 13).
This type of chord of a sixth with a third in between became
common in written polyphony as did progressions of several such
chords in parallel motion approaching a cadence or end of line.
Faburden made a mannerism of this progression, creating what
the English would call a "merry" sound. In France the technique,

EXAMPLE 13: FABURDEN

called *fauxbourdon*, featured melody on top, rather than in the middle, with the parallel sixth below. The middle part was added in performance and moved constantly at a fourth below the melody. This technique was often used for settings of the regular Office chants and of psalms and texts such as the *Magnificat* and the *Te Deum*. Its practical consequence in music history was the emergence of a new style of three-part writing, where the three voices assume more equal importance and create a more unified, consonant sound.

French composer Guillaume Dufay (1400–1474) used *fauxbourdon* very successfully in a cycle of hymn settings in which verses of *fauxbourdon* were sung alternately with chant. French composers also experimented with alternating solo groups (one singer on each of two parts) with chorus (several singers on each of three parts), phrase by phrase throughout a Mass setting or other piece of service music.

The number of polyphonic Masses increased in the later fourteenth and early fifteenth centuries. Chant was variously used, most importantly in the *"cantus firmus"* or "cyclical" Mass, where every movement was constructed around the same chant melody. This process forged the five sections—*Kyrie, Gloria, Credo, Sanctus,* and *Agnus Dei*—into a unique artistic unity.

The cyclical Mass found its most important location in the ducal chapel, or private place of worship for a duke and his family. Often designed as an architectural gem and decorated with priceless paintings and tapestries, the chapel contained all the necessary religious necessities for the carrying out of services—chaplain, acolytes, choirmaster, choir of men and boys, vestments, and elaborate furnishings. The duke saw to it that he and the liturgy were surrounded by the best that his means could procure. In this milieu the cyclical Mass found a home suitable to its rich, ultra-sophisticated nature. Several composers famous for their connections not only with cathedrals but also with the royal chapels of the time were Johannes Ockeghem (1420–1497), Jacob Obrecht (1452–1505), and Josquin des Prez (1440–1521).

The royal patronage of musical activity created a demand for music. With the perfecting of movable type by Johann Gutenberg, liturgical books with plainchant notation were printed by 1473. Part books were the norm for publications—one volume for each voice or part.

Throughout the period now designated as the Renaissance (roughly 1450–1600) efforts were made to bring music into closer alliance with the literary arts. It became the rule to follow the rhythm of speech and not to violate the natural accentuation of syllables. Composers sought to dramatize the content of the text, to make it more directly appealing and meaningful to listeners. Overall there was a rededication to human as opposed to spiritual values. Besides salvation after death, fulfillment in life was now seen as a desirable goal and musical forms reflected this ideal.

Music of the German Reformation

When Martin Luther nailed his ninety-five theses to the door of the Schlosskirche at Wittenberg in 1517, he did not intend to initiate a movement toward a Protestant church that would be completely separate from Rome. Even after the break, the Lutheran Church kept much traditional Catholic music, both plainsong and polyphony. Luther was a singer and composer of some skill who admired Franco-Flemish polyphony, especially the works of Josquin des Prez. Believing strongly in the educational and ethical power of music, he wanted the entire congregation to participate in the service music with words altered to conform to his own vision on certain theological points. The Latin language was often retained alongside many additions in German.

The most distinctive and influential musical innovation of the Lutheran Church was the strophic congregational hymn called the "chorale." These songs were intended for congregational singing in unison, without harmonization or accompaniment but, like the plainchant, lent themselves to later enrichment through harmony and counterpoint. Luther himself wrote the words and probably the melody to the well-known *Ein' feste Burg ist unser Gott* ("A mighty fortress is our God"). The Gregorian hymn *Veni Redemptor gentium* became *Nun komm' der Heiden Heiland* ("Come, Savior of the Gentiles") and the Easter sequence *Victimae Paschalis laudes* was the model for *Christ lag in Todesbanden* ("Christ lay in the bonds of death"). Chant had come to be associated with the large chorus, as opposed to the especially trained ensemble.

The Counter-Reformation

The Roman Catholic Church reacted to the defection of its northern brethren by beginning its own program of internal reform known as the Counter-Reformation. A special council, meeting intermittently in Trent in northern Italy from 1545 to 1563, worked to formulate and pass measures aimed at purging the church of abuses and laxities. With regard to music, concern was voiced that the Mass had been profaned when it was based on secular melodies. Complicated polyphony made it difficult to understand the words of the texts and instruments were being used carelessly and inappropriately. A codicil from the Council of Trent describes the music henceforth to be used in the Mass:

> All things should indeed be so ordered that the Masses, whether they be celebrated with or without singing, may reach tranquilly into the ears and hearts of those who hear them, when everything is executed clearly and at the right speed. In the case of those Masses which are celebrated with singing and with organ, let nothing profane be intermingled, but only hymns and divine praises. The whole plan of singing in musical modes should be constituted not to give empty pleasure to the ears, but in such a way that the words be clearly understood by all, and thus the hearts of the listeners be drawn to desire of heavenly harmonies, in the contemplation of the joys of the blessed. They shall also banish from church all music that contains, whether in the singing or in the organ playing, things that are lascivious or impure.[3]

According to legend, it was the composer Giovanni da Palestrina (1525–1594) who saved polyphony from the council's condemnation by composing the six-voice *Missa Papae Marcelli* ("Pope Marcellus Mass") that was reverent in style and did not obscure the words of the text. Palestrina spent his whole professional career as church musician in Rome, first as choirmaster of the Cappella Giulia at St. Peter's in 1551 and during the following forty years as choir master at St. John Lateran and Santa Maria Maggiore. During the latter part of his life, he was given the task of revising official chant books so as to purge them of the "barbarisms, obscurities, contrarieties, and superfluities" that had come into them, said Pope Gregory XIII, "as a result of the clumsiness or negligence or even wickedness of the composers, scribes, and printers."[4] This work, continued by others after Palestrina's death and finally appearing as the Medicean edition of the *Gradual* in 1614, remained in use until the definitive Vatican Edition of 1908 was published by the Benedictines of Solesmes.

More than any other composer, Palestrina was able to capture the essence of the sober, conservative aspect of the Counter-Reformation. Purity was his obvious intent and it could be seen in the contrapuntal elegance and consistency of his compositions. The individual voice parts have an almost plainsong-like quality, with motion that is mostly stepwise, with short infrequent leaps. His melodic lines are easily singable, though tightly woven, and display a marked regularity of rhythm, also characteristic of his style.

Palestrina wrote more than 250 motets and related types of music (hymns, Magnificats, psalms) but especially Masses, 105 in all. His reserved and mystical kind of polyphony became the new official music of Catholicism and influenced contemporary composers such as Tomas Luis de Victoria (1548–1611) and Orlando di Lasso (1537–1594), as well as many others yet to come.

The last of the great Catholic Church composers of the sixteenth century was William Byrd (1543–1623). Writing in England, a Protestant (Anglican) state where Catholic music was banned, he nevertheless succeeded in composing three Masses (one each for three, four, and five voices) that are among the finest ever written by an English composer.

Byrd's motets, for which he is also justly famous, were intended mainly for private devotional gatherings, but he designed two books of Gradualia (1607) for liturgical use. In the dedication to one of them he paid tribute to the power of scripture to fire the imagination.

I have found there is such a power hidden away and stored in those words [of scripture] that—I know not how—to one who meditates on divine things, pondering them with detailed concentration, all the most fitting melodies come as it were of themselves, and freely present themselves when the mind is alert and eager.[5]

Byrd's extraordinary ability to draw together the threads of religious polyphonic music and to apply them imaginatively is pointed out by Grout and Palisca[6] and illustrated by them with a fragment of Byrd's motet *Tu es Petrus* quoted below. Note that at the words *aedificabo Ecclesiam meam* (I will build my church), the composer portrays the building of the church by a theme that rises an octave, first through a third and then step by step. A long pedal note on the word *petram* (rock) is a musical pun on the name of the apostle *Petrus* (Peter), upon whom, like a rock, Christ would build his church.

EXAMPLE 14: SIXTEENTH CENTURY MOTET BY WILLIAM BYRD

From Donald J. Grout and Claude V. Palisca, *A History of Western Music* (New York: W. W. Norton & Company, 1996), 263.

Later Developments

With the beginning of the seventeenth century we will conclude our brief overview of musical innovations that could be said to have developed directly from Gregorian chant, the treasure held for a thousand years by the Benedictines. Through their daily worship and devoted practice, the monks and nuns continued to provide the *cantus firmus* for all the new music created by church musicians and in society in general. Because of their efforts, the liturgy of the Opus Dei and the Mass, as well as anthems to honor Christ and the Holy Mother, were and have continued to be part of the consciousness of composers throughout the West. Musical forms created in the monasteries—organum, tropes, sequences, hymns, motets, and liturgical dramas—had taken firm root and were available for future elaboration.

After 1600 the whole spectrum of musical style was transformed in an effort to make a clear, distinct, forceful impact on the listener. Choral music tended to lose its mystical aspect with the belief that listeners could be reached only through insistent, exaggerated overstatement, a tendency which, by its sheer exteriority, was no longer monastic.

The Gregorian repertory and early polyphony had been performed by the unaccompanied human voice with the addition of organ interludes. However, this changed more and more, as instruments either dubbed or were used in place of the vocal line. Keyboard instruments, played by a single performer, were capable of reproducing, all by themselves, the harmonic fabric of the music. Trio sonatas, works for instruments alone to be played at appropriate moments in the church service, became frequent after 1650. Music drama was slowly transformed into the sacred concerto where voices and instruments were combined; in the hands of secular composers the opera was born, creating a lavish combination of soliloquy and dialogue, placed in an elaborate setting of continuous music and elaborate staging.

During the next century composers sought an ever more varied, flexible style; each work was to have its own individual character and means of expression. As variety increased, so did the need for larger, stronger forms such as the concerto and the symphony. Musical expression had moved away from modal scales and harmonies and now showed a clear sense of key. The relationship of each chord to this tonal center became the most important element of style.

By 1800 musicians were no longer writing either for church or court, nor were they employed by them. Rather, they addressed themselves to an international bourgeois concert-going audience and were paid through box office and publisher.

Nearly all composers of repute, however, tried their hand at elements of the traditional liturgy—Mass, *Te Deum*, *Magnificat*, *Stabat Mater*, Passion (narration of the crucifixion of Jesus), anthems to Christ or the Virgin Mary. A perfect example of the musical achievement and synthesis of the early eighteenth century was the extraordinary work of Johann Sebastian Bach (1685–1750). When polyphonic music first began to develop, composers were mainly content to add one layer of music at a time usually over a base chant or secular melody, or to blend a dance rhythm with a lyric to produce a two-part song. With Bach there was a striking development: not only was each part beautiful in its own right, but Bach linked them all so as to form a complete harmonious whole. A composer-performer able to do virtually anything with his material, Bach could take simple dance rhythms and turn them into elaborate fugues, suites, or variations. He made music that joined art and science, moving people's hearts and disciplining their minds in a way that had never before been achieved on such a scale or with such intensity.

George Frederic Handel (1685–1759), a contemporary of Bach, was a master of melody and broadly sweeping choral music. As much as Bach was studious and thorough, summing up the past, Handel anticipated the future with his tremendous energy and enterprising spirit. It was he who perceived that the opera was becoming too elaborate, expensive, and less appreciated by audiences in England. His solution was to establish the oratorio, where sacred words were substituted for secular, and costly sets were eliminated. Handel's *Messiah* established the oratorio as the national art form in England.

Nineteenth-Century Revival of Chant

In chapter 5 we described the determined efforts made at the Benedictine Abbey of Solesmes to restore the chant and bring it back to its rightful place in Catholic liturgy. The work of these monks came to the attention of some of the most well-known composers of the late nineteenth and early twentieth centuries.

Claude Debussy (1862–1918) heard Gregorian chant at the church of St. Gervais in Paris and had a revelation concerning its importance while he was in Rome. He was so inspired by its beauty that he made a pilgrimage to Solesmes in August of 1894. The direct result can be heard in his opera *Pélléas and Mélisande*, completed in 1902, where certain arias and harmonies are inspired by Gregorian modality.

Gabriel Fauré (1845–1924) studied music at the Ecole de Musique Classique in Paris. Founded by the composer Louis Niedermeyer (1802–1861), this school was a major center of plain-chant studies. Fauré's Requiem consciously broke with the dramatic aesthetic inherited from the Requiems of Berlioz and Verdi. Its calm portrayal of death—not as terror-filled, but rather as a happy deliverance—strongly recalls the corresponding Gregorian liturgy.

Maurice Duruflé (1902–1986) went a step further in his Requiem, seeing chant as the source and origin of his melodic inspiration. As he later wrote:

> Completed in 1947, this Requiem is based entirely on the Gregorian themes from the Mass for the Dead. Either the words have been respected in their entirety, with the orchestra writing merely supporting or commenting on them, or I allowed myself simply to be inspired by them... Generally speaking I tried, above all, to immerse myself in the particular style of the Gregorian melodies, forcing myself to reconcile, as far as possible, the Gregorian rhythms as fixed by the Benedictines of Solesmes with the demands of modern meter. As for the musical form of each of the sections of this Requiem, it was inspired, in general, by the form of the liturgy.[7]

Strong influences stemming from Gregorian chant can also be heard in the compositions of a number of other Catholic musicians who, unlike the Romantic composers of their time, saw their works as instruments for spiritual transformation rather than as opportunities for personal expression and aggrandizement. Anton Bruckner (1824–1896), a devout Catholic and Austrian composer, placed particular emphasis on the vocal line, as was always typical of traditional church music. His polyphony is straightforward and comprehensible, the music in service to the words conveyed.

For Olivier Messiaen (1908–1992), the sole purpose of his transcendent, spiritual music was to turn people to Christ. Whereas the classical development of music moved rhythm away from the freedom of chant toward the measure-restricted "beat," Messiaen worked to free it again. In particular he rediscovered a medieval device called "isorhythm" where unique patterns of chords, pitches, and rhythms revolved around each other. By avoiding metrically defined phrases and patterns of stressed and unstressed beats, these isorhythmic "wheels within wheels" did away with any sense of meter. The title of Messiaen's glorious "Quartet for the End of Time" is a pun on words where "the end of time" also means the end of the "beat"!

This extraordinary composition was written in 1940–1941 when Messiaen, who had volunteered for the hospital corps, was overtaken by the German advance near Nancy, transported across Germany to Silesia, and imprisoned in Stalag 8a. Having no food and little clothing, he nevertheless had a knapsack filled with musical scores. The camp commander discovered this unusual captive and allowed him to continue composing. Messiaen completed the Quartet while in prison and, with the help of his fellow inmates, performed it in January 1941 in the prison camp, before more than four thousand prisoners and their guards.

It is amazing, under such circumstances, that Messiaen was able to compose a work having nothing to do with war. The Quartet is entirely about a vision of heaven where violence and despair do not enter; there is no darkness, vengeance, or rage but only a sense of light, transcendence, and joy—qualities so characteristic of the Gregorian repertory.

The influence of chant, and of its Benedictine practitioners, continues today. The stunning success of the 1993 recording, *Chant*, sung by the Benedictine monks of Santo Domingo de Silos and the popularity of many other outstanding recordings made by Benedictine monks and nuns illustrate a strong intergenerational interest in a more healthy and sane sort of music. As will be further explained in chapter 8, the influence of chant can also be strongly seen in the work of composers who do not try to "create an effect" but rather step aside so that the voice of Spirit may most effectively be heard.

The Organ and Church Bells

It would be entirely remiss to leave our discussion of Benedictine influence on the development of music without mentioning their contribution to the arts of making and playing the organ as well as the casting and use of church bells.

Although the chant itself is unaccompanied by any instrument, it has long been part of church tradition to introduce organ interludes into the liturgy. Benedictines were the first organists and they were also the first organ makers.

As early as the eighth century the organ was used by monastic teachers in Western Europe as a way to illustrate the mathematical laws underlying pitch relationship. Small instruments, extending to only one octave, were also designed especially to teach chant.

Organs made their way into the most important abbeys of France, Italy, and England during the tenth and eleventh centuries. Their spread was slow, since the instruments were costly. However, if one can believe certain documents, there was a colossal organ in the monastic cathedral of Winchester, England, around 950. According to the monk Wolstan, who described it, the organ had four hundred pipes and twenty-six bellows. The instrument was activated by sixty-six men and played by two organists at once. It was said that, when all its various voices sounded together, the impression was terrifying!

The period from 1100 to 1400 saw great activity in the design and use of organs. Most monastic churches had an instrument that was played at ceremonies and festival occasions by skilled Benedictine organists—a tradition that reached its height in the seventeenth and eighteenth centuries. Organs were manufactured by monks before the work was taken over by other artisans. Dom François Bedos de Celles, Benedictine of the congregation of Saint-Maur, one of the most famous erudite Benedictine congregations, wrote the most celebrated work that has ever appeared on the art of making organs. After long years of research, he published his three volumes on the classic manufacture of organs in 1776–1778. The volume was reedited in 1849 and 1903 and during the first part of the twentieth century it appeared in facsimile.

The first ecclesiastical use of bells, in the days before watches and clocks, was to announce the hours of the Opus Dei and the Mass. Bells were a practical necessity in every monastery from as early as the time of St. Benedict. The ringing of bells was and still is the call to prayer, letting the monks know that the time has come for them to leave their other tasks and return to the oratory or chapel. The quarter hour single toll marks the time but also reminds each individual monk to lift a short prayer to God.

Bells from the parish church traditionally announced the services, alerted the town to imminent danger, tolled to solemnize a time for mourning, or rang in joyful profusion to signal public celebration. Each bell had not only its own name, given to it during a "baptism" ceremony, but also its unique voice or tone appropriate to its message—the curfew, a warning to return home and extinguish fires and lights for the night; the passing bell, used in monasteries to call the community to the bedside of a dying member; the *tocsin*, or alarm bell; the *salva terram*, providing protection in times of storm or danger; the *classicum*, several bells ringing at once to announce a solemn feast or the presence of honored guests.

Bells were manufactured by the Benedictines in Italy starting in about the year 530, when Benedict established his monastery at Montecassino, a location near the pre-Christian bronze-casting center of Nola. At Montecassino the Benedictines developed the art of casting large bells, making sketches of their profiles and writing specifications for their materials and weights. As the Order spread, it built foundries in its monasteries elsewhere and became the first large-scale supplier of bells to Christian institutions throughout Western Europe.

Church bells are instruments that cannot be ignored. Their sound resonates within our own substance, reminding us to awaken to their call and respond to their message.

8
Benedictine Gifts

"Seek out peace and pursue it."
St. Benedict

If art can be said to be the reflection of its age and period, music is certainly its echo. This is not simply a passive echo, for music reverberates in the minds and hearts of its listeners, creating an ethos that powerfully affects their physical health, their creative abilities, and their spiritual life, or lack thereof. Between the raucousness of heavy metal and the calm luminous melody of plainchant lies a whole octave of Being. The ancient Greeks were right—music is still the regulator. Whether we admit it or not, we are all subject to a particular drummer. Our relative freedom lies in choosing the song.

More than anything we need a way to make God's presence real, a part of our experience. Everywhere we turn, people are searching, running from workshop to workshop, trying each new fad in the ever-expanding market of spiritual opportunism. We read many books, engage in activities galore, and stress ourselves even more to overcome the tension and busyness that troubles us in the first place. Given the prevailing state of affairs in society and in ourselves, the contemplative tradition of the Christian Church may seem remote and difficult to access. Many of us have only a passing acquaintance with the holy fathers and mothers of years gone by. Our interiorization of the sacred scriptures remains superficial, often caught in a mixture of fundamentalism, scholarly attempts to explain everything, or simple neglect and indifference.

Meeting us in our situation of need, the Benedictines can offer us three precious gifts: first, the chant itself; then, inspiration for the contemporary composer of sacred music; and, finally, the example of a way of being that will help us, more and more, to find rest in God's holy presence and, therein, find a measure of peace.

The Holistic Benefits of Chant

Chant is not a gift that the Benedictines have created, since its roots go back we know not where or when—no doubt to the whisperings of the Holy Spirit itself into the ears of countless generations of anonymous composers. What the Benedictines have done, however, is to preserve this treasure in the most effective way possible, which is by making it part of their lives.

For those interested primarily in receiving holistic benefits, listening to chant with one's full attention brings a balanced and peaceful state of mind and body; chant is healthful and energizing. Research by the French doctor Alfred Tomatis has shown that there are sounds known as "discharge" sounds, which fatigue the listener, and "charge" sounds, which give energy and health.[1] Charge sounds are rich in high frequencies, whereas discharge sounds are of low frequency. Dr. Tomatis put an oscilloscope to the sounds of Gregorian chant and found that it contains all the frequencies of the voice spectrum, roughly 70 to 9,000 hertz, but with a very different envelope curve from that of normal speech. The monks sing in the medium range—that of a baritone—but due to the unity and resonance of the sound, their voices produce rich overtones of higher frequency. It is these high tones, mainly in the range of 2,000 to 4,000 hertz, that charge the brain with energy.

It has always been part of the traditional understanding that sound is causative or formative, meaning that it has power to create certain effects in spirit, mind, and body. Indeed, sound literally matters; it has the power to give shape to materials. Swiss physicist Hans Jenny performed a number of astonishing experiments illustrative of the effect of sound on inert matter. He placed substances such as iron filings, drops of water, soap bubbles, and lycopodium powder (spores of club moss) on a diaphragm and subjected them to a variety of sounds. The result was a series of flowing, changing patterns of great beauty and complexity. These patterns have been recorded and are shown in Professor Jenny's videotapes and two-volume presentation entitled *Cymatics* (the science of the way the properties of a medium change under the influence of vibration).[2]

Human beings are much more sensitive than inert matter to what they hear! We have five senses, five groups of organs (hearing, touch, sight, taste, and smell) through which we are in contact with external reality. We relate to this reality in three ways: intellectually, emotionally, and actively. These modes constitute the basis for the formation of the personality, which is envisaged as being oriented along three great currents of psychic activity— intellectual, emotional, and motor. Each of these is associated with a psychosomatic relation with a body location where it appears to evoke a resonance. Of course the somatic seat of these functions cannot be precisely located, yet popular language, often vivid and direct, speaks of head, heart, and guts in this connection. This is a rather simple, yet profound observation. Such a framework provides a useful and practical model, grounded in a robust common sense and informed by keen psychological observation through the centuries. It can be developed into a very fine instrument for self-observation as well as for gaining insight into others' behavior.

The music we hear is primarily apprehended by one center, emotional, intellectual, or active, although all music contains elements of each. Repeatedly acting on that center, it imparts its quality to our personality; it provides energy to the center to which it is directed. As far as Gregorian chant is concerned, it does not serve primarily to set us thinking or incite us to action. Instead, it provides relief from the surfeit of ideas and activities that fatigue and weaken us, giving us something of great importance—nourishment for the heart.

In the same way that what one thinks is not a matter of indifference, the sounds one produces and listens to are also of vital import. When we attend a concert or turn on the radio or CD player, we need to ask ourselves the essential questions, "What effect is this sound or this music having on my mind, my heart, and my body?" "Where do I feel it and what is it doing?"

The Practice of Chant

Those who wish to go beyond just listening and penetrate more deeply into the musical treasure house of chant actually practice it. In order for this practice to have the desired effect—which is to assist us to draw near to God—it must be taught by musicians skilled in its rules and practice and cognizant of its spiritual value. When this is the case, a door is opened to contemplative practice and singers are led to a very different experience of the Christian life.

Rembert Herbert, who served for many years as cantor of St. James's Episcopal Church, Capitol Hill, Washington, D.C., and from 1986 to 1999 as director of the Schola Cantorum of New York, provides an extremely clear and insightful explanation of the far-reaching benefits of chanting in his book *Entrances: Gregorian Chant in Daily Life*.[3] He points, in particular, to the fact that chant is both a diagnostic tool and a cure for the state of mental agitation in which we often find ourselves. Even a few minutes of its practice can point out to each of us our lack of attention and focus, our tendency to be everywhere except in the present moment—the only place where God is to be found. Chant shows us that our human ability to perceive what is most important and most deeply true is far from consistent and changes frequently as we move from apathy to a deeper awareness and inspiration and back again.

Gregorian chant, sung in Latin or in vernacular language, has rules that have been consciously designed to disarm, to disorient, and to awaken. This is to be expected, since any spiritual practice worth its salt contains some element of offense to the everyday world. In one way or another it says "no" to doing things in "any old way" or as we, personally, might prefer.

The singer of chant learns to be self-directed but in full awareness of the whole group. Even when the liturgy calls for what might seem to be a "solo performance," the simplicity and straightforwardness of the melodic line will soon reveal any traces of personal ego appearing in the sound. Each individual needs to be aware of the fact that the sound emerges from silence, rises as on the crest of a wave, and then returns to silence. The singer must be continuously alert, making a conscious, non-mechanical, relaxed effort to stay with the group.

In chanting the liturgy, diction needs to be precise—a practice that cuts across habits of sloppy speech and articulation—so that the word, which is the point of the practice, may be clearly heard. In an age when the expression of the individual's every thought and feeling on any and all subjects is highly esteemed, here the effort is precisely to make no attempt to sing "with expression" or to "create a melodic line." Herbert puts it this way:

> Rather than a "line," a chant melisma should be thought of as a succession of still moments not coming from anywhere, not going anywhere. The choir should sound as if it could stop at any instant in the melisma and remain at that moment forever. The melisma is a kind of study in the paradox of stillness in motion. The voices move but give the effect of not moving. At any moment in the melody, the "present moment" is the only moment of consequence.[4]

Chant is purposely "poor" in the expression of individual personality and artistry. There is nothing in it to excite the superficial emotions or the senses and, for this reason, it brings deep refreshment and rest. Its overriding lesson is that even when singing a chant's most demanding melismas, singers need to practice a simple, prayerful approach. The text should be allowed to speak in its own voice without interference from the singers.

When chant is skillfully practiced, it becomes much more than a tool for mirroring our mental and emotional state. It has the effect of stilling the mind and opening the heart. In particular, it awakens a deeper intelligence and receptivity in responding to the words both of scripture and of the church fathers.

Sacred texts have the capacity to speak to us according to the occasion and our need. If our minds are literal, then one meaning is provided. If we move, through disciplined singing of chant and through prayer, to a deeper level, scripture meets us there with a more profound symbolic meaning.

In chanting the liturgy, people are often puzzled by a phenomenon known as centonization or "patchwork," whereby the texts for the chants of the Proper are taken from widely separated parts of the Bible, so as to create a new mini-text, with its own special focus. The centonization serves to identify the major themes of the particular day or feast and makes the individual aware of the many scattered instances where it is mentioned or alluded to, literally or prophetically. Rembert Herbert explains that when the awakened and stilled intelligence of the individual meets the words of scripture, these words are then found to be symbols with particular meaning to each person:

> The central idea behind the symbolic use of the Bible is that all of scripture speaks a consistent message in a consistent language. The message lies on a plane above the historical context of any given passage and is constant throughout the centuries. From the point of view of the true author, the Holy Spirit, writings which seem to us many centuries apart are simultaneous, one sentence right with another, Old and New Testaments created "together," in a timeless present. All these writings

speak of transcendent and unchanging realities—the laws and being of God, the inner nature of the human person reaching for God, the mysteries of Christ and his Church.[5]

In what is essentially a monastic view, Herbert goes on to point out:

In order to enter the Fathers' world, we must become comfortable with this allegorical or symbolic language. We must first of all accept at least the possibility that every word of scripture is true in an exact symbolic sense, and that symbolism is the necessary language of the inner world of the spirit. The forces that operate in that world shape our lives, and yet the language of contemporary culture gives us only the most awkward terms with which to name them. To enter that world, we must also adjust our habits of mind to accommodate multiple meanings, multiple types of meaning, the often unexpected behavior of inner forces, and different ways of "receiving" meaning.[6]

In the contemplative tradition it is typical to find the sacred text delivered in small, very compact pieces, as it is in chant. As opposed to longer texts designed to offer explanation and pleasure to the intellect, these short pieces allow the singer time to more closely examine and inwardly digest the words. He or she then perceives that there are a number of equally valid interpretations of the text, that it is, in fact, speaking to each person in an intensely personal way. The process is that of moving progressively from the literal to the symbolic meaning and even beyond that to a place where the words are perceived as pure energy or consciousness.

The practice of Gregorian chant and the reading of the writings of the church fathers go together. Chant is a musical interpretation of scripture and the writings are verbal interpretations. The point of engaging in both is not merely to find more hidden meanings behind the literal meaning. Rather, it provides us with a glimpse of a totally different reality, expressed by Thomas Merton as "the divine life itself."

Chant has been cited by the Second Vatican Council's *Constitution on the Sacred Liturgy* as especially suited for the Roman liturgy. It is to be hoped that it will continue to be reintroduced in the churches, along with its rich heritage of polyphonic music, and that the secular clergy in the parishes will increasingly choose the finest, most expert musicians, in tune with the Gregorian tradition, to lead their choirs. Precision and accuracy are of the greatest importance if the spiritual gift of the chant is to be fully realized in our services of worship and within us personally.

Inspiration for a New Song

A thought-provoking article on what makes music sacred was written in 1999 for *Crisis* magazine by Robert R. Reilly.[7] In it, Reilly points out that the traditional role of music—"to make the transcendent perceptible and, in so doing, exercise a formative ethical impact on those who listen to it"—has been lost for most of the twentieth century. In fact, the very opposite has been at work. Composers have been eager to imitate the sound of the crowd in their effort to be reflective of what is rather than to create and give directives as to what should be. Exercising a kind of positive feedback, they have reproduced what is emerging from society—its violence, confusion, and despair. The effect of this picking up and amplifying wave after wave of deleterious sound has produced heavy metal and other destructive kinds of music which, if we subscribe to the traditional view, will lead to more and more crime in our streets and homes.

Reilly states that a major problem contributing to the sense of discord and disorientation characteristic of so much of modern music is its loss of tonality, a method of composition wherein the notes and chords of a composition are related to a central key note. He points out that tonality began to be disregarded at the same time that God disappeared from widespread cultural awareness. This "death of God" became as much a problem for music as it was for philosophy. He expresses the dilemma in this way:

> If there is no pre-existing, intelligible order to go out to and apprehend, and to search through for what lies beyond it—which is the Creator—what then is music supposed to express? If external order does not exist, then music collapses in on itself and degenerates into an obsession with techniques. Any ordering of things, musical or otherwise, becomes purely arbitrary.[8]

Citing an example, Reilly recalls the work of Arnold Schoenberg (1874–1951) who created a system of twelve-tone composition with specific rules—no pitch could be repeated, with the exception of immediate repetition, until all twelve notes had been used. This process avoided any particular note's becoming an anchor for the ear, which could then recognize what was going on in the music harmonically. With this "serial" type of approach, the music loses any sense of movement away from a state of tension or relaxation, any feeling of motion through crises and conflicts to resolution. The overall effect is one of complete disorientation. Musical composition mirrors the state of society in general—a condition where the difference between one thing and another has been blurred and discrimination, for all intents and purposes, is lost. The musical idea is that people are so immersed in atonal music that discords come to be heard as concords. Schoenberg is quoted as saying that he was "conscious of having removed all traces of a past aesthetic...cured of the delusion that the artist's aim is to create beauty."[9]

French composer Pierre Boulez (b. 1925) carried the concept further by applying the total rejection of the past not only to tonality but to every aspect of music—pitch, duration, tone production, intensity, and timbre. Countering the classical view of music as a thing of beauty, designed to lift people up into something greater than themselves, he declared, "Once the past has been got out of the way, one need think only of oneself."[10]

For American composer John Cage (1912–1992), the point was to reject all organization and strive for the non-mental. He composed noise through chance operation, by rolling dice, or drew notes according to the irregularities on the composition paper. (One could say that his closest approach to Benedictinism was the composition of 4'33" [1952] in which musicians sit silently with their instruments for precisely four minutes and thirty-three seconds!) Whereas Schoenberg often watched TV while composing music according to formulae predetermined by himself, Cage is said to have sliced up tape recordings, jumbled them, pieced them together, and presented them as music. Chance and blind selection replaced consciousness of intent as principles of composition.

Fortunately, these attempts were not of long duration. A number of extremely innovative musicians such as Arvo Part (Estonian, b. 1935), Krzysztof Penderecki (Polish, b. 1933), and David del Tredici (American, b. 1937) were among those who began to draw the line, moving away from a musical world where only dissonance and atonality were acceptable. American George Rochberg (b. 1918), the leader of the twelve-tone school of composition in the United States, renounced this view and expressed his return to more traditional forms in this way:

> The pursuit of art is much more than achieving techni-cal mastery of means or even a personal style; it is a spir-itual journey toward the transcendence of art and the artist's ego...I am turning away from what I consider the cultural pathology of my own time toward what can only be called a possibility: that music can be renewed by regaining contact with the tradition and means of the past, to re-emerge as a spiritual force with re-activated powers of melodic thought, rhythmic pulse, and large scale structure; and, as I see it, these things are only pos-sible with tonality.[11]

A recent article in the *New York Times* speaks of American Alan Hovhaness (1911–2000) as rarely transgressing the bound-aries of conventional tonality and as emphasizing the impor-tance of the human voice. He is quoted as saying,

> There is a center in everything that exists. The planets have the sun; the moon, the earth. All music with a cen-ter is tonal. Music without a center is fine for a minute or two, but it soon sounds all the same.

I've used all the techniques including the 12-tone technique. But I believe melody is the spring of music. The human voice was the first instrument, and I believe that all the different instruments are voices as well. So I want to give them melodies to sing. I think melodically and without melody, I don't have much interest in music.[12]

Given the desire manifested by contemporary composers to reconnect sacred music with tradition, we can certainly ask what Benedictines, as bearers of the Christian contemplative tradition, might offer in the creation of "a new song"—an appropriate sacred art form for the new millennium. To clarify their possible contribution, we can reflect for a moment on the two meanings of the word "tradition." On one hand, it refers to a set of established ideas and practices passed from generation to generation. In music this means those musical forms that the culture understands—modality, tonality, counterpoint, fugue, canon, symphony, sonata, etc.—and that are collectively remembered. The musician has the choice, of course, of composing mechanically entirely according to pre-established rules.

But as an anonymous writer has said, "To be a guardian [of the great spiritual work] signifies two things: the study of and practical application of the heritage of the past, and secondly continuous creative effort aiming at the advancement of the work. For the Tradition lives only when it is deepened, elevated, and increased in size. Conservation alone does not suffice at all . . ."[13]

Therefore another meaning of "tradition" refers not to the form passed down from years gone by but rather to its living spirit. This tradition is not something to be learned from reading scores or listening to recordings but from practices that put one into direct contact with the Source that inspired the form in the first place.

A beautiful example of this is provided by the work of Benedictine oblate Therese Schroeder-Sheker, who has pioneered the work of music thanatology, which she defines as "a palliative medical modality employing prescriptive music to tend the complex physical and spiritual needs of the dying."[14] Schroeder-Sheker centers her activities at St. Patrick Hospital in Missoula, Montana, where she is academic dean at the School of Music-Thanatology and founder/director of the Chalice of Repose Project. Since 1992 the Chalice of Repose has trained a large and specialized team of music-clinicians who provide musical deathbed vigils in many different hospital, hospice, and home settings.

Schroeder-Sheker explains that the vocal and harp music offered is never the same, even if people are dying of the same disease. The prescriptive music is designed in the moment to match the dynamic physiological changes taking place in the patient's nervous, respiratory, circulatory, and metabolic systems. It is always delivered live, because it is made specifically appropriate to the changing physical, emotional, and spiritual state of the one who is dying.[15]

The music thanatologists who attend at the bedside are skilled both musically and spiritually. They are able, through their own practice of presence and caring, to provide an "anointment with sound" that is extremely helpful not only to the patient but also to the grieving family members.

Trained in medieval studies, Schroeder-Sheker has taken much of her inspiration from monastic medicine as it was practiced in the tenth-century Abbey of Cluny.[16] She states that infirmary practices for the care of the dying developed there clearly predate modern palliative medicine by eight hundred years. Attention was given to the physical, emotional, mental, and spiritual pain that might impede or prevent one from a blessed death. The monastic infirmary at Cluny left detailed accounts, in particular, of the *musical* ways in which the dying were tended.

The Gregorian chant repertory continues to inspire the compositions created today by Chalice of Repose practitioners. Schroeder-Sheker sees these melodies as "the language of love," and adds that they "carry the flaming power of hundreds of years and thousands of chanters who have sung these prayers before."[17]

Benedictines remind us of transcendence, of the fact that life as experienced through the senses is designed to teach us about and lead us to a world beyond, which is, in fact, more real, and eternal. Music which they could inspire would not be music that stops here in this world but, like the ancient chant, would bring one to a place where everything is true and free from sorrow. Like chant, and like icon paintings, the music would move beyond the strictly individual toward a more universal portrayal of that which is beautiful and good. In it we would hear something divine, something participating in the song of the angels.

This form of art would contain elements of the symbolic and the discrete. It would not tend to force itself on the listener or draw from him or her any particular, pre-determined response. Jean Leclercq has expressed this thought with regard to literature but it applies equally well to music:

> Art can be but the reflection of spiritual experience, never a means for provoking it in the writer or in the reader. Sought after for its own sake, it forms a screen

between the author and ourselves, the author becomes
an aesthete, we are spectators, and there is no longer
any communion in love of Truth.[18]

Contemporary American composer and Benedictine oblate
Johannes Somary has expressed the attitude appropriate to the
composers of sacred music: they should do their work "on their
knees."[19]

Sacred music as understood by the Benedictines is "the word
of God singing." Whatever music is to be expressed is actually
contained in the word and is there for those prepared and willing
to listen. Like St. Gregory the Great, composers must open their
ears to the sounds of the dove whispering in their ears. They must
spend time living and interiorizing the text they wish to use.

Even though Benedictines have always been called upon to
be extremely flexible, adapting themselves to the locale and the
situation in which they find themselves, they never make excessive accommodation either to the time or to the mores of the
moment. They are able to allow the shape of the chalice to
change somewhat, while retaining the essence within. Composers too are not asked to become slaves to traditional forms,
nor to totally reject them. Rather, they are called upon to gather
up all their formal training and expertise and then to move aside
in order for Spirit to work through them.

This process is eloquently described by English composer
John Tavener (b. 1944) in his book *The Music of Silence: A
Composer's Testament*,[20] which is a series of conversations
between Tavener and editor Brian Keeble. Tavener characterizes modernism in music as being the antithesis of communication that has "an unparalleled vocabulary of techniques and formulae. But at the same time it has a parallel lack of symbols,

metaphysics, orientation, beauty, and divinity."[21] He goes on to say:

> Only human beings are in the image of God and only human beings stand on the border, poised between angel and animal. This points to the human capacity to make signs—to make things which re-present realities of a higher dimension in things. We are creatures that point to our Creator. The modernist has already set *himself* up as "creator," he has wiped God out of the picture. It is just a dialogue between him and the synthesizer. God is wiped out, humanity is wiped out and so is the cosmos . . . it is everything goes and anything goes.[22]

The composing itself does not call for a great deal of cerebration. According to Tavener, it is associated with a lack of labor and earthly care, and with total subjection to the word of God. Writing music seems to him like "looking and looking and looking at God, and then copying his work. The work has been done—now glorify."[23]

The second gift, then, that the Benedictines provide is the example of listening to the silence, of creating a place where God may speak. Composers who learn from their example will create a New Song—a work of transcendent beauty.

The Way of Devotion

The increasing number of Benedictine oblates and Benedictine lay organizations who follow the Rule bear witness to reception today of the third gift that the Order can offer to us—a model for contemplative life. Even if we do not consider ourselves singers or composers, we can still receive and benefit from this invaluable source of spiritual knowledge.

To help us to understand the "Way of Devotion" modeled for Christians by the Benedictine and other monastic orders, but also present in other spiritual traditions, we will return to the octave. Recall that this is not simply a visual model but one that is made of sound, a medium that, as we saw in the liturgy, the ancients considered eminently appropriate for conveying spiritual knowledge. The diagram is to be read from bottom to top:

THE WAY OF DEVOTION

Do Complete union with God
    Interval—Friendship with God
Si Service to the whole creation

La Prayer of the heart

Sol Worship

Fa Obedience
    Interval—Reflection
Mi Awakening

Re Singing praise

Do Hearing

The octave begins, as Benedict so clearly advises in the prologue to the Rule, with hearing. We are to listen "with the ear of the heart," in other words, with full intention and awareness, so that the activity becomes much more than the sheer taking in of sound impressions. This is the beginning of the octave, the *Do*, the point where the aspirant becomes aware of the spiritual tradition, in whatever way is open.

Benedict is extremely precise about the second step. As we have seen, he does not simply suggest singing the Lord's praise but, following scriptural directives, actually prescribes it "seven times during the day and once at night" (i.e., an octave). The chant is the first prayer wherein the person learns to listen to the sound of his or her own voice, in the context of the community effort. The song provided is one that will serve to quiet the body and mind and assist the singer to ascertain the state of his or her human instrument at the moment of practice. The octave moves forward on *Re* with this beginning of self knowledge.

The act of singing has the effect of opening up space in the mind and heart. With this comes the first awakening, represented by the note *Mi*—an appreciation of the tradition, an acknowledgment of the beauty inherent within it, and a reverence for its teachers.

The other essential practice, that of *lectio divina*, requires the individual's own effort and is present to fill the octave interval. Here one must consciously recall or recollect whatever of importance the spirit has known or made conscious in the past, so that the treasures may go deep and not simply be forgotten. At this point the individual begins to perceive some of the sweetness so characteristic of the monastic approach. The way, in its fullness, is not yet perceived, and yet abundant light is present.

With the note *Fa*, more is required. The hearing that was there from the beginning becomes more precise and refined. The individual comes to a fuller realization that God's will for his or her life is right in front, present in the exigencies and relationships of everyday life. It is then a question of increasing obedience to the inner directives abundantly supplied by these demands and challenges. For the monastic, obedience is extended to the following of directions from lawfully elected superiors and working cooperatively with others in the Order.

Worship is represented by the *Sol,* the dominant, of the octave. It is placed at the center and affects all steps below and above. At this point the individual experiences greater and greater unity between thought, word, and deed. Worship is not simply the carrying out of the liturgy, although this is done with increased fidelity. It becomes the consecration, the making sacred, of all aspects of life. Benedict refers to this when he speaks of welcoming guests as if they were Christ himself and treating the tools of manual labor as if they were articles placed on the altar.

With the ascent of the octave, the way is characterized, more and more, by a drawing near to God. The step *La* is connected here with prayer, in the same way that it is associated with the Lord's Prayer in the Mass. Whereas the prayer expressed by the chant at step 2 is more external and communal, here it is internalized and intensely personal. There is continual gratitude for all God's wondrous gifts and a subtle change in one's attitude toward work takes place. One fully realizes that, each time work is done with full conscious awareness, the activity itself becomes prayer. The attention is at rest completely with the work and nowhere else. All the activities of life are transformed and assume a transcendent dimension. This rising octave is not to be seen so much as a moving up as a deepening of rest in the Spirit. Each new step includes the preceding ones. The process is a widening of the spectrum rather than a floating toward an imaginary heaven.

A person prepared by the preceding steps is a man or woman in waiting, ready and able to do the Lord's bidding at each and every moment. At this step, the note *Si*, there is no turning back in providing service to the whole of creation through the returning of fine for coarse.

A radiant example of this step is given by Andrew Harvey[24] as he describes precious hours he spent with Benedictine monk Bede Griffiths, when Griffiths was on his deathbed. Harvey considered this monk not only as his closest personal friend but as the most holy person he had ever met. He remarks that Fr. Bede never considered his own life and spiritual development as fully achieved. Until the moment of his dying breath, prayer was always on his lips. At the point when his vision had failed and where he was no longer able to recognize his many visitors, he nevertheless took the head of each one in his hands and, weeping in gratitude for their love and caring, offered them his blessing.

The interval between *Si* and *Do* is filled by and with the grace of God. The wall of personal ego is no longer present, so it is said, and the person radiates peace and tranquility in all circumstances of life. This step is sometimes referred to as "friendship with God" because, more and more, the man or woman is seen to mirror the divine image of Christ. He or she is not far from the octave's completion, full union with God, which is the aim and purpose of human life.

St. Benedict presents the Way of Devotion as one of loving and peaceful living. He warns us in his Rule that the way "is bound to seem narrow to start with. But, as we progress in this monastic way of life and in faith, our hearts will warm to its vision and with eager love and delight that defies expression we shall go forward on the way of God's commandments."[25] This is the invitation and the promise of the third gift.

Notes

Chapter 1

1. There are also a few Benedictine communities representing other Christian denominations in the United States: Anglican: St. Gregory's at Three Rivers, Mich.; Lutheran: St. Augustine's House, Oxford, Mich.; and Methodist: St. Brigid of Kildaire, Collegeville, Minn.

2. The Most Rev. Marcel Rooney, O.S.B., former abbot primate of the worldwide Benedictine Confederation and chancellor of St. Anselmo University, Rome, personal letter, August 16, 1999.

3. Thanks to Sr. Donald Corcoran, O.S.B. (Cam.), Transfiguration Monastery, Windsor, N.Y., for conversation about chant.

4. Willi Apel, *Gregorian Chant* (Bloomington: Indiana University Press, 1990), 39.

5. Ibid., 39.

6. Ibid., 40.

7. The liturgical year is presented here as beginning with Advent, as it is represented in the *Liber Usualis*, in the *Gregorian Missal*, and in the readings of the church.

8. *Saint Benedict's Rule*, trans. Patrick Barry, O.S.B. (York, England: Ampleforth Abbey Press, 1997), 102–3.

9. For further information on the significance of the musical octave, see Boris Mouravieff, *Gnosis: Etude et commentaires sur la tradition ésotérique de l'orthodoxie orientale* (Neuchâtel, Switzerland: Les Editions de la Baconnière, 1969).

10. I thank Abbot Patrick Barry for bringing this event to my attention. It is taken from Bede's *Ecclesiastical History of the English People* (New York: Penguin Books, 1991), chapter 18, 234–35.

11. I am greatly indebted to R. John Blackley, director of the Schola Antiqua of Baltimore, Md., for information about proportional chant. More on this subject may be found at www.scholaantiqua.net.

12. Particular thanks to Fr. Augustin Curley, O.S.B., Newark Abbey, Newark, N.J., for sharing with me notes from his lectures on the cultural contributions of the Benedictines.

13. In the fifteenth and sixteenth centuries there were very strong monastic reforms in Italy (the Cassinese Congregation of St. Justina of Padua) and in Spain. Then in the seventeenth century came a strong reform at St. Vannes in France, home of the Maurists, the ultimate scholar monks whose tradition undoubtedly influenced and made possible much that happened in the nineteenth century at Solesmes.

14. "La parole de Dieu qui chante" is an expression used by the Benedictines of the French Abbey of Saint-Pierre de Solesmes in their videotape: *Le Chant grégorien*, Université de Nantes, 1994.

Chapter 2

1. From *Gregory the Great: The Life of Saint Benedict*, Commentary by Adalbert de Vogüé, O.S.B. (Petersham, Mass.: St. Bede's Publications, 1993), 164.

2. *Saint Benedict's Rule*, trans. Patrick Barry, O.S.B. (York, England: Ampleforth Abbey Press, 1997), vi.

3. Ibid., vi.

4. Benedict's monastery at Montecassino was destroyed by the Lombards in 568, some twenty years after his death. (It was destroyed again in 1944 in one of the fiercest battles of World War II.) In 717 it was restored and in 741 Pope Zachary sent to Petronax, its abbot, what he called "the Rule that the blessed Father Benedict wrote with his own

holy hands." In 787 the Holy Roman Emperor, Charlemagne, who was sponsoring a great reform of the Benedictine monasteries, requested that an exact copy of Benedict's autograph (original) be brought back to him at Aachen (Aix-la-Chapelle). The manuscript at St. Gall is either the same one ordered by Charlemagne or a very close copy thereof.

5. *Saint Benedict's Rule*, 17.

6. Ibid., 19.

7. Ibid., 21.

8. Patrick Barry, "The Inherent Role of Beauty in the Monastic Tradition," unpublished paper, St. Louis Abbey, St. Louis, Mo., October 1999.

9. Ibid.

10. I owe appreciation to Sister Catherine Goddard Clark, Abbot Primate Jerome Theisen, and the authors of the Monastery of Christ in the Desert for their insightful articles on Benedict and Gregory appearing on the Internet at http://www.christdesert.org/pax.html.

11. Pearce Cusack, *An Interpretation of the Second Dialogue of Gregory the Great*, Studies in the Bible and Early Christianity: 31 (Lewiston, N.Y.: E. Mellen Press, 1993).

12. Herbert Thurston, "Use of Numbers" in the Internet version of the *Catholic Encyclopedia* at http://www.newadvent.org/cathen.

13. Thurston, "Symbolism" in the Internet version of the *Catholic Encyclopedia*.

14. Demetrius Dumm, O.S.B., *Cherish Christ Above All* (Mahwah, N.J.: Paulist Press, 1996), 40.

15. *Saint Benedict's Rule*, 1.

16. Ibid., 6.

17. Barry, "The Inherent Role of Beauty in the Monastic Tradition."

18. Ibid.

19. Ibid.

20. Dumm, *Cherish Christ Above All*, 8.

21. Jeremy Driscoll, O.S.B., "Monastic Culture and the Catholic Intellectual Tradition," in *Examining the Catholic Intellectual Tradition*,

ed. Anthony J. Cernera and Oliver J. Morgan (Sacred Heart University, Fairfield, Conn., 2000), 55–73.

22. The Manquehue Movement is an extended Benedictine community in Santiago, Chile. Some of its members are oblates and the others maintain varying degrees of commitment. Their main work is in education and has led to the founding of San Benito College (1982; 1,500 pupils); San Lorenzo College (1986; 600 pupils), San Anselmo College (1995; 500 pupils), and San Mauro College (opened in March 2001). Boys and girls, ages four to eighteen, receive an education inspired by Benedictine life and the values of the gospel.

23. Quoted with permission from the Manquehue Apostolic Movement, *The Little Rule for Oblates*, November 1998 version. Section 7, "The *Acogida*—Welcome and Affirmation in Christ."

24. Abbot Primate Marcel Rooney, letter of August 16, 1999.

25. See Jack and Marcia Kelly, *Sanctuaries: A Guide to Lodgings in Monasteries, Abbeys, and Retreats of the United States* (New York: Bell Tower, 1991).

Chapter 3

1. Acts 2:42.

2. *Saint Benedict's Rule*, 28.

3. Psalm 118 (119):164.

4. Psalm 118 (119):62.

5. Psalm 118 (119):164.

6. *Saint Benedict's Rule*, 99.

7. *Antiphonale Monasticum* (Tournai, Belgium: Desclée & Co., 1934), 872.

8. Abbaye St. Pierre de Solesmes, *Liber Cantualis* (Sablé-sur-Sarthe, France, 1983), 81–82.

9. Unpublished translation by Fr. Ralph Wright, O.S.B., St. Louis Abbey, St. Louis, Mo.

10. Numerous translations of Ambrose's famous hymns, among them *Veni redemptor gentium*, "Come Redeemer of the Nations," and *Jesu, nostra redemptio*, "Jesus Our Redeemer," still appear in the *1982 Episcopal Hymnal*.

11. Matthew 18:20.

12. Vatican Council II, *Constitution on the Sacred Liturgy*, 83.

13. For a fuller explanation of the role of music in the medieval world view, see *Chant: The Origins, Form, Practice, and Healing Power of Gregorian Chant*, by Katharine Le Mée (New York: Bell Tower, 1994).

14. See Boris Mouravieff's study of oriental Orthodoxy, *Gnosis, études et commentaires sur la tradition ésoterique de l'orthodoxie orientale* (Neuchâtel, Switzerland: Editions de la Baconnière, 1969), vol. 1, chapters X and XI.

15. Robert Taft, S.J., *The Liturgy of the Hours in East and West* (Collegeville, Minn.: The Liturgical Press, 1986), 352.

16. A full presentation of the year-long liturgy is given in the *Liber Usualis*, ed. Benedictines of Solesmes (Tournai, Belgium: Desclée and Co., 1952), 317–1080.

17. In the present-day Roman Catholic calendar, the liturgical year concludes with the Solemnity of Christ the King, the Sunday following the Thirty-third Sunday in Ordinary Time.

18. Psaml 2:11.

19. Psaml 47:7.

20. Psaml 138:1.

21. *Saint Benedict's Rule*, 28.

Chapter 4

1. Psalm 115:1.

2. Willi Apel, *Gregorian Chant* (Indianapolis: Indiana University Press, 1990), 39.

3. Ibid., 40.

4. Ibid., 50.

5. Monks of the Abbey of Saint-Pierre de Solesmes, *Le Chant Gré-gorien: La parole de Dieu qui chante* (Nantes, France: Université de Nantes, 1994). Video in French.

6. Jos. Smits Van Waesberghe, *Gregorian Chant and Its Place in the Catholic Liturgy* (Stockholm: The Continental Book Company, 1947), 14.

7. Quoted by Willi Apel in *Gregorian Chant*, p. 267, as being from Augustine's explanations of Psalms 99 and 32.

Chapter 5

1. Georges Duby, *The Age of the Cathedrals*, trans. Eleanor Levieux and Barbara Thompson (London: Croom Helm, 1981), 73.

2. Therese Schroeder-Sheker, "Music for the Dying," *Noetic Sciences Review* (Autumn 1994), 33.

3. *The Letters of Hildegard of Bingen*, trans. Joseph L. Baird and Rodd K. Ehrman (New York: Oxford University Press, 1994), 78–79.

4. Nancy Fiero, C.S.J., Mount St. Mary's College, Los Angeles, Calif., Internet article *Hildegard of Bingen: Symphony of the Harmony of Heaven*, http://www.uni-mainz.de/~horst/hildegard/music/music.html.

5. Saint Hildegard of Bingen, *Symphonia: A Critical Edition of the Symphonia armonie celestium revelationum (Symphony of the Harmony of Celestial Revelations)*, with introduction, translations, and commentary by Barbara Newman (Ithaca, N.Y.: Cornell University Press, 1988).

6. *Meditations with Hildegard of Bingen*, trans. Gabriele Uhlein (Santa Fe, N.M.: Bear & Company, 1983), 93–96.

7. Thanks to Sr. Monica Laughlin, O.S.B., professor of music at the College of St. Scholastica, Duluth, Minn., for her informative article "An Ancient Heritage Lives," which appeared in *Pathways*, the Newsletter of the Benedictine sisters, Duluth, Minn. (Spring 1996), vol. 7, no. 3.

8. *A Benedictine Book of Song, I* (Collegeville, Minn.: The Liturgical Press, ca. 1979).

9. *A Benedictine Book of Song, II* (Collegeville, Minn.: The Liturgical Press, ca. 1992).

10. See Sr. Cecile Gertken's *Sunday and Weekday Office Hymns of the Liber Hymnarius*, published in 1987 by St. Benedict's Monastery, St. Joseph, Minn.

11. Alan J. Hommerding, "Sent Forth by God's Blessing: Roman Catholic Hymn Text Writers after Vatican II," *The Hymn* (October 2000), vol. 51, no. 4.

12. Sr. Delores Dufner, O.S.B., *Sing a New Church* (Portland, Ore.: OCP Publications, 1994). In this book, each hymn appears first as a poem, with commentary below that includes scriptural references and themes as well as suggestions for liturgical use and performance. On the facing page the same text appears with its recommended melody. The hymnbook is available from Sisters of the Order of St. Benedict, 104 Chapel Lane, St. Joseph, MN 56374 or from OCP Publications, 5536 NE Hassalo, Portland, OR 97213.

13. Thanks to Brother Philip Fronckiewicz, O.S.B., for his letter and conversation about Weston Priory and its music. For a catalogue of recordings and accompanying sheet music, contact Weston Priory, 58 Priory Hill Road, Weston, VT 05161.

14. For a fuller discussion, see *RB 1980: The Rule of St. Benedict*, ed. Timothy Fry, O.S.B., Imogene Baker, O.S.B., Timothy Horner, O.S.B., Augusta Raabe, O.S.B., and Mark Sheridan, O.S.B. (Collegeville, Minn.: The Liturgical Press, 1981), 131–36.

15. Jean Leclercq, O.S.B., "Otium Monasticum as a Context for Artistic Creativity," *Monasticism and the Arts*, ed. Timothy Verdon (Syracuse, N.Y.: Syracuse University Press, 1984).

16. Ibid., 65.

17. Ibid., 76.

18. Jean Leclercq, O.S.B., *Love of Learning and the Desire for God* (New York: Fordham University Press, 1961), 75.

19. For information on HMML, thanks to the writers of Saint John's Internet web page: http://www.csbsju.edu/hmml/intro/history.htm.

Chapter 6

1. Saint Anselm, *The Prayers and Meditations of Saint Anselm with the Proslogion* (New York: Penguin Books, 1973), 110.

2. Patrick Barry, O.S.B., "The Inherent Role of Beauty in the Monastic Tradition," unpublished paper, St. Louis Abbey, Mo., October 1999.

3. Pope John Paul II, General Audience of November 29, 1995: "Mary shows us God's respect for women."

4. Luke 1:38.

5. Luke 1:42.

6. Luke 2:19.

7. Luke 2:29–32.

8. Luke 2:35.

9. Luke 2:40.

10. John 19:25.

11. Pope John Paul II, encyclical letter *Redemptoris Mater*, "On the Blessed Virgin Mary in the Life of the Pilgrim Church," March 25, 1987, #26.

12. Sally Cunneen, *In Search of Mary* (New York: Ballantine Books, 1996), 150.

13. Ibid., 121–22.

14. Michael O'Carroll, *Theotokos, A Theological Encyclopedia of the Blessed Virgin Mary* (Wilmington, Del.: Michael Glazier, Inc., 1986), 8–9.

15. Pope John Paul II, *Redemptoris Mater.*

Chapter 7

1. Abbot Patrick Barry, O.S.B., translates the quote, written by St. Gregory the Great about St. Benedict in the *Second Book of the Dialogues* as "well aware of his ignorance and wisely remaining uneducated." He points out that the quote distinguishes Benedict from the

normal university "dropouts" of today, who are often confused about what they are doing or arrogant and contemptuous of what they are rejecting. It is almost as though St. Gregory anticipated this modern phenomenon and pointed out that Benedict was clear-headed, knew exactly what he was doing, and showed great wisdom in turning away from the education offered in Rome.

2. From Richard H. Hoppin, *Medieval Music* (New York: W. W. Norton & Company, 1978), 222.

3. Quoted by Donald J. Grout and Claude V. Palisca in *A History of Western Music* (New York: W. W. Norton & Company, 1996), 250.

4. Grout and Palisca, *A History of Western Music*, 251.

5. Ibid., 262.

6. Ibid., 263.

7. From liner notes by Lucie Kayas, written for compact disc *Fauré Requiem*, Opus 48 and *Duruflé Requiem*, Opus 9, Sony Essential Classics, 1995.

Chapter 8

1. Tomatis's work is described by Bradford S. Weeks, M.S. in "The Physician, the Ear, and Sacred Music," an essay in *Music Physician for Times to Come*, ed. Don Campbell (Wheaton, Ill.: Quest Books, 1993), 46.

2. Dr. Hans Jenny, *Cymatics: Bringing Matter to Life with Sound*, video by Macromedia, Box 1223, Brookline, MA 02146.

3. Rembert Herbert, *Entrances: Gregorian Chant in Daily Life* (New York: Church Publishing Inc., 1999).

4. Ibid., 78.

5. Ibid., 23.

6. Ibid., 97.

7. Robert R. Reilly, "Is Music Sacred?" *Crisis Magazine* (September 1999): 27–31.

8. Ibid., 29.

9. Ibid.

10. Ibid., 30.

11. Ibid., 31.

12. *New York Times*, "Alan Hovhaness, a Composer Whose Vast Catalog Embraced Many Genres, Dies at 89," Friday, June 23, 2000, A21.

13. Anonymous, *Meditations on the Tarot: A Journey into Christian Hermeticism*, trans. Robert Powell (Warwick, N.Y.: Amity House, 1985), 608.

14. Therese Schroeder-Sheker, "Music for the Dying," *Noetic Sciences Review* (Autumn 1994): 32–36.

15. Therese Schroeder-Sheker, "Shaping a Sanctuary with Sound: Music-Thanatology and the Care of the Dying," *Pastoral Music* (February–March 1998): 26–41.

16. Therese Schroeder-Sheker, "Death and the Chalice of Repose Project," *Lapis two*, New York Open Center, 83 Spring Street, New York, NY 10012.

17. Ibid.

18. Jean Leclercq, O.S.B., *The Love of Learning and the Desire for God* (New York: Fordham University Press, 1982), 263.

19. Johannes Somary, in a private conversation in June of 1999.

20. John Tavener, *The Music of Silence: A Composer's Testament* (London: Faber and Faber, 1999).

21. Ibid., 96.

22. Ibid., 97.

23. Ibid., 140.

24. From *Radiant Heart*, by Andrew Harvey (Boulder, Colo.: Sounds True audio learning courses, 1999).

25. *Saint Benedict's Rule*, Prologue, 5.

For Further Study

A Benedictine Book of Song, I. Collegeville, Minn.: The Liturgical Press, ca. 1979.

A Benedictine Book of Song, II. Collegeville, Minn.: The Liturgical Press, ca. 1992.

Apel, Willi. *Gregorian Chant.* Bloomington: Indiana University Press, 1990.

Cunneen, Sally. *In Search of Mary.* New York: Ballantine Books, 1996.

de Waal, Esther. *A Life-Giving Way: A Commentary on the Rule of St. Benedict.* Collegeville, Minn.: The Liturgical Press, 1981.

de Waal, Esther. *Living with Contradiction: An Introduction to Benedictine Spirituality.* Harrisburg, Pa.: Morehouse Publishing, 1989.

Duby, Georges. *The Age of the Cathedrals.* Translated by Eleanor Levieux and Barbara Thompson. London: Croom Helm, 1981.

Dufner, Delores, O.S.B. *Sing a New Church.* Portland, Ore.: OCP Publications, 1994.

Dumm, Demetrius, O.S.B. *Cherish Christ Above All.* Mahwah, N.J.: Paulist Press, 1996.

Flanagan, Sabina. *Hildegard of Bingen: A Visionary Life.* London: Routledge, 1989.

Gregory the Great. *The Life of Saint Benedict.* Commentary by Adalbert de Vogüé, O.S.B. Petersham, Mass.: St. Bede's Publications, 1993.

Grout, Donald J., and Claude V. Palisca. *A History of Western Music.* New York: W. W. Norton & Company, 1996.

Herbert, Rembert. *Entrances: Gregorian Chant in Daily Life*. New York: Church Publishing Co., 1999.

Hoppin, Richard H. *Medieval Music*. New York: W. W. Norton & Company, 1978.

Kelly, Jack, and Marcia Kelly. *Sanctuaries: A Guide to Lodgings in Monasteries, Abbeys, and Retreats of the United States*. New York: Bell Tower, 1991.

Lachman, Barbara. *The Journal of Hildegard of Bingen*. New York: Bell Tower, 1993.

Leclercq, Jean. *Love of Learning and the Desire for God*. New York: Fordham University Press, 1961.

Le Mée, Katharine. *Chant: The Origins, Form, Practice, and Healing Power of Gregorian Chant*. New York: Bell Tower, 1994.

Pelikan, Jaroslav. *Mary through the Centuries*. New Haven, Conn.: Yale University Press, 1996.

RB 1980: The Rule of St. Benedict. Edited by Timothy Fry, O.S.B., Imogene Baker, O.S.B., Timothy Horner, O.S.B., Augusta Raabe, O.S.B., and Mark Sheridan, O.S.B. Collegeville, Minn.: The Liturgical Press, 1981.

Saint Benedict's Rule. Translated by Patrick Barry, O.S.B. York, England: Ampleforth Abbey Press, 1997.

Steindl-Rast, David, O.S.B. *The Music of Silence*. San Francisco: Harper Collins, 1994.

Taft, Robert. *The Liturgy of the Hours in East and West*. Collegeville, Minn.: Liturgical Press, 1986.

Tavener, John. *The Music of Silence: A Composer's Testament*. London: Faber and Faber, 1999.

Verdon, Timothy Gregory. *Monasticism and the Arts*. Syracuse, N.Y.: Syracuse University Press, 1984.

Index